# Painting Flowers on Rocks

# Painting Flowers
# on Rocks

## LIN WELLFORD

**NORTH LIGHT BOOKS**
CINCINNATI, OHIO

## ABOUT THE AUTHOR

Lin Wellford readily acknowledges her good fortune in receiving early encouragement that fostered her interest in art. Pen-and-ink sketches and watercolor landscapes played a part in her evolution as an artist, as did three years' study of advertising design at the University of Florida. Moving to the Arkansas Ozarks opened the door to her career as a "rock artist" and has provided an ongoing source of inspiration. As with her previous books, *The Art of Painting Animals on Rocks*, *Painting More Animals on Rocks* and *Painting Houses, Cottages and Towns on Rocks*, she hopes this book will inspire others to see the creative possibilities in rocks and perhaps discover hidden talents within themselves.

Wellford lives in Green Forest, Arkansas, with her husband, Klaus. They are the parents of three daughters.

Other fine North Light Books are available from your local bookstore, art supply store or direct from the publisher.

11   10   09   08   07      13   12   11   10   9

**Library of Congress Cataloging in Publication Data**

Wellford, Lin
  Painting flowers on rocks / Lin Wellford.
      p.   cm.
  Includes index.
  ISBN-13: 978-0-89134-945-7 (pbk.: alk. paper)
  ISBN-10: 0-89134-945-6 (pbk.: alk. paper)
  1. Stone painting. 2. Acrylic painting. 3. Flowers in art. I. Title.
TT370.W455   1999
751.4′26—dc21

98-41076
CIP

Edited by Roseann Biederman
Production edited by Amy J. Wolgemuth
Designed by Mary Barnes Clark
Production coordinated by Kristen Heller

**fw**
F+W PUBLICATIONS, INC.

## DEDICATION

For my parents, Nancy and Marion Wellford, who provided the
ways and means for a happy, creative childhood.

With thanks to David and Katie Hanshaw, Monte and
Suzanne Villines, Beth Stafford, Bill and Nancy Riddle, and
especially Fayrene and Gaylord Farmer
for the use of their interiors and gardens.

# Table *of* Contents

*Painting Flowers on Rocks*

# Introduction

When I painted my first rock years ago, I certainly never imagined the many magical possibilities this humble material offered. Even now, whether I'm working on a furry little creature, a vine-covered cottage or a vase of flowers, the thrill of making something beautiful from an ordinary rock never wears off. I love knowing that every piece I paint is a one-of-a-kind creation; while rocks may be common and plentiful, each and every one is unique. A particularly fine rock, or one with an unusual shape, can still get my creative juices flowing. And I never tire of hearing people exclaim, "I can't believe this is just a rock!" Flowers and houseplants are among nature's most vivid and appealing creations, so it's hardly a surprise that people continue to be drawn to them as subjects for their own artistic expression. Rock painting offers a whole new spin on this age-old art form, capturing the beauty of flowers and plants in three dimensions!

Since many of the projects in this book require simply mastering one basic flower or leaf shape at a time, painting flowers on rocks may be the most accessible rock art of them all. Whatever your skill level, you will quickly discover that compared to a flat surface, it's far easier (and a lot less intimidating) to paint something that already has shape. Rocks offer an exciting and inexpensive painting surface for beginners as well as for those seasoned artists in search of a new challenge.

Another advantage is that while flat art requires expensive framing to be finished, rock artwork is ready to display as soon as the paint dries. Show it off anywhere you might place a live plant—on a coffee table, fireplace mantel, windowsill or desk. Rock creations require neither light nor care, so they can brighten those corners where living plants would never survive. Painted rocks are guaranteed not to wilt or drop their petals when left untended for months, even years. And unlike plastic or silk flowers and foliage, rock paintings won't fade or grow dingy. They're a snap to clean with just the swipe of a damp cloth.

Best of all, painted rock flowers and plants make ideal gifts for housewarmings, birthdays, anniversaries or as personalized thank-yous. The fact that they're carefree and wiltproof makes them a perfect decoration for a shut-in's bedside. Is there any office that wouldn't benefit from the presence of an attractive painted plant? And who wouldn't welcome a handcrafted nosegay of bright blossoms that does double duty as a paperweight. Whatever the occasion, these unique works of art are bound to attract both comment and admiration. Perhaps the highest compliments I received were from the butterflies and bees who persistently buzzed around my rock art blooms while I was photographing finished pieces outdoors. Who says you can't fool Mother Nature?

"I can't believe it's just a rock!" Like mini-murals, painted rock pieces will fool the eye.

## GETTING STARTED

One of the most exciting aspects of painting flowers and plants on rocks is that almost any size, shape and kind of rock can be used: the smoothest and roundest of river-tumbled rocks, the most irregular of fieldstones, even those chunky rocks often found at building sites and along country roads.

Once you've trained yourself to pay attention, you'll begin to see wonderful rocks all around you. Flat, shale-type rocks may work loose from eroding layers where roads have been cut into hillsides. Rounded rocks line riverbeds and ocean beaches, while chunky rocks and fieldstones can be found along many roadsides. In a pinch, you can even browse through a rock yard where builders buy their rocks by the ton. Most businesses will be happy to sell you a few rocks for a pittance. On occasion, they've even let me take the ones I've selected at no charge.

Needless to say, finding good rocks to paint is easy. With all the various colors and types of plants and flowers to choose from, deciding what to paint first may be the most difficult task you face. Every project I try leaves me with new appreciation for the diversity and vivid hues that surround us in the natural world. Pore over those gardening catalogs that start to arrive in the mail in the midst of winter. Analyze the shapes and textures that characterize different plants and shrubs. This will help you to visualize what kinds of rocks would work best for specific subjects. Flowers, such as roses and sunflowers, can be painted as single blooms. Others, such as pansies and petunias, look best in clumps or masses. Tulips and daffodils work well on tall, narrow rocks, while hostas call for large, flat fieldstones. Sprawling caladiums are perfect for angular pieces.

Fieldstones, usually fairly flat, offer dramatic angles that often mimic live plant shapes.

Chunky, side-of-the-road rocks may be the most common and easy to find.

Water-tumbled rocks offer smooth contours in a surprising number of shapes and sizes.

*Painting Flowers on Rocks*

Some rock shapes even resemble flower-filled pots, vases and baskets.

The only rock types I avoid are those with surfaces so rough or bumpy that creating details on them is nearly impossible and those so thin that they are subject to breaking.

## SUPPLIES

Once you've gathered some potential flower rocks, you'll need a few inexpensive, easy-to-find supplies.

### Paints

- I prefer acrylic paints in the little plastic bottles for ease of use and good adherence. They are widely available, inexpensive and come in a wide range of colors. Although you may use any type of acrylic paint you have on hand, including artist-quality or crafter-type paints, there are many projects in this book that you may be tempted to display outdoors. For that reason, I recommend using DecoArt brand Patio Paints, a new acrylic paint that has been specifically formulated to resist weathering (now widely available in arts and crafts stores). However, if you are interested in creating decorative pieces solely for indoor display, regular acrylics are just fine.

Designed to resist weathering, these acrylic paints will help ensure a longer life for your painted creations displayed outdoors.

This simple design was executed on a Colorado rock sent to me by a friend.

## Brushes

Most of the projects presented here can be done with a handful of common brushes. If you already have brushes, experiment with them before investing in a whole new set. If you're not yet a painter, I suggest starting with the following brushes:

- For fine lines and detail, my choice is Loew-Cornell's 7050 series scriptliner brush, no. 0 or 1. It has a nice long bristle that can carry a lot of paint, and it holds a sharp point despite the challenging texture of this medium.
- A wide, flat brush in size ¾-inch or 1-inch (19mm or 25mm) is useful for covering large areas quickly.
- Filbert brushes in various sizes (no. 4 is my favorite) will make some petal and leaf painting easier.
- A few angle shader brushes in small and medium sizes, ½-inch (13mm) and smaller, are indispensable for daisy and rose petals. I especially like the Loew-Cornell 7400 series, which, like the liners, hold their shape despite abuse.
- A few other handy brush types, including medium and small round brushes and perhaps a short detail brush.

Just a few good brushes will handle all of the projects presented here.

*Painting Flowers on Rocks*

## Other Supplies

- You can use regular chalk for sketching on your initial designs, but white charcoal pencils make finer lines.
- Fine-point permanent markers (such as Sharpie) are also handy for layouts as well as for signing and dating your finished pieces.
- Wood fillers, such as 3-in-One brand Plastic Wood or Leech Real Wood, may be used to correct an uneven base or to fill in a hole or crack.
- Clear acrylic spray finish will enrich your colors and protect the surface of your rocks.
- Pieces intended for display on scratch-prone surfaces should be fitted with a scrap of felt glued to the bottom to create a buffered base.

## A Few Last Words

Keep in mind that it is impossible to ruin a rock. Since this painting surface is usually free, there's no need to feel intimidated. Plunge right in and experiment, giving yourself permission to play and explore. You don't need any artistic training to master this medium—just a willingness to try and the ability to follow directions. If you already have your own techniques for painting various flower types, feel free to substitute them for my directions.

My hope is that this book will serve as a starting place. Once you begin to see the possibilities, there is literally no end to the beautiful things you can create.

Basic supplies include an assortment of acrylic craft paints, a white charcoal pencil, marker, wood filler and acrylic spray finish.

Painting Flowers on Rocks

# How to Paint
# Primroses

ompact, colorful primroses make ideal subjects for rock painting. Their overall shape conforms neatly to fit on any rounded rock, and their uncomplicated blossoms are easy to master. Use your primrose creations singly as paperweights or desk art, or cluster them for a striking display. Although real primroses are attractive and popular, they don't thrive in many climates, so these painted versions may be the only way some people will ever enjoy the quaint, old-fashioned charm of primroses.

Look for a plump, rounded or oval river rock that is at least the diameter of your open palm, but no larger than the span of an outstretched hand. Make sure the rock surface is clean and dry before painting.

This rock is a perfect size and shape for a tight cluster of flowers.

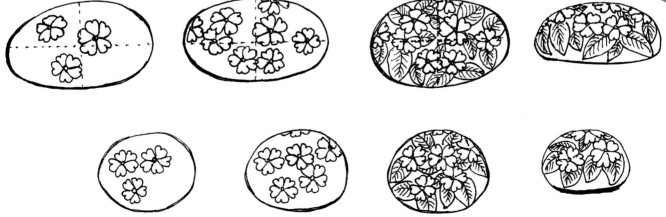

Sample layouts for a larger oval and a smaller round rock.

## 1 Base Coat

A dark background is best for setting off flowers and foliage.

Mix a loaded brush full of Sprout Green paint into a puddle of black to soften the color. Or, you may prefer to use a deep shade of brown instead. Either way, for best results, the base coat should be dark. Paint the entire upper surface of the rock, leaving only a small oval on the underside where you'll sign and date the piece when finished. Allow this paint to dry before moving on to the next step.

## 2 Layout

It will help to divide your rock's top surface into quarters; use chalk or a white charcoal pencil to draw perpendicular lines marking the quarters. Individual primrose blossoms consist of five heart-shaped petals connected by a small round center. Using chalk or white charcoal pencil, fit the first blossom, measuring 1½″ (3.8cm) across, into the upper right quadrant of your rock. Sketch two more full flowers in the two adjacent sections in varying positions to form an irregular triangle. For variety and a more realistic look, tuck partially overlapped flowers alongside two of the three main flowers, then sprinkle three or four more blossoms around the upper perimeters, allowing some to brush petals with others, while others stand apart. Set aside the lower third of the rock for foliage.

Work around the outside edges next, sketching in simple, broad, oval leaves with tapered ends. Alter the angle and size of the leaves as you tuck them in below your blossoms. Fill in any large spaces between the blossoms on top with the tips of leaves, or perhaps part of a leaf as shown.

A deep base coat provides a dramatic backdrop.

Large blooms are easier to paint and make for a more attractive result.

Primrose petals step by step.

*Painting Flowers on Rocks*

# 3 Paint the Petals and Leaves

Using a no. 6 or 8 round brush or a no. 4 filbert brush, fill in the flower outlines with Sunshine Yellow. Light colors may require two coats for complete coverage. Leave the center circle in each blossom unpainted. While the petals are drying, fill in the leaf outlines with Sprout Green. Remember to paint in the partial leaves that show between the flowers as well.

# 4 Paint the Flower Centers

Leaving the unpainted spot in the center, paint a star shape in each flower using a small round brush and Golden Honey paint lightened a shade by adding Sunshine Yellow. These stars may be somewhat irregular since they'll blend in with the yellow petals. The stars should be neater, however, when painted over contrasting petal colors such as red, purple or white.

Switching to a script liner, mix a very small amount of the same gold color with an equal amount of Sprout Green. Dab this sparingly into the center of the flower, allowing traces of dark undercoat to show around the edges for emphasis and added depth.

Pale colors, such as yellow, gold or white, may require two coats for solid coverage. Leave a small, unpainted circle in the center of each bloom.

Fill in all of the leaf outlines with straight Sprout Green.

Use feathery strokes, working out from the center with a contrasting mixture of Golden Honey brightened with Sunshine Yellow.

With a touch of Sprout Green added, the same golden yellow becomes a subtle accent in the center.

*How to Paint Primroses*

# 5 Petal Details

Start with a small amount of Pinecone Brown softened and lightened with Sunshine Yellow. With the tip of a script liner, use this color to define the individual petals along with a few shorter lines to accent the star-shaped gold center of each flower. This soft brown can also be used to delineate any place where one flower overlaps another, as well as to create shadows around the overlapped area. Pinecone Brown, with a touch of black to darken it, may be used for added emphasis anywhere petals need even greater definition.

Soft brown lines delineate individual petals, accent the golden star-shaped center and create the illusion of shadows on overlapped petals.

Darker brown will separate overlapping petals, but use it sparingly.

*Painting Flowers on Rocks*

# 6 Leaf Details

Start with Sprout Green, deepened with just enough black to make a green that's darker than the leaves but brighter than the base coat. Use a medium flat or filbert brush to create shadows along the upper portions of the leaves so the flowers appear to be overhanging and shading them. Extend a darker line down the center of the leaf as well, leaving the outer edges and the tips lighter green.

Next, mix a small amount of Sprout Green with enough Sunshine Yellow to create a brighter green. Use this color and a script-liner brush to outline the outside edges of each leaf with a small, flicking motion. The outline should be slightly jagged rather than smooth and straight. Stroke in a center spine accent on each leaf, and extend narrow rib lines down both sides. To give the leaves a hint of sheen, add in some shorter, narrower strokes of this bright green along the outer edge of the leaves wherever light might fall.

Shading in all the upper portions of the leaves will make them recede, helping the flowers to stand out.

Lighter green edges, spines and ribs redefine and add realistic detail to the leaves.

Lightened with a trace of Sunshine Yellow, the same green can suggest a soft sheen when drybrushed or scribbled along the leaf edges.

# 7 Finishing Touches

Look your piece over. At this point you may notice areas where the petals could use a bit more definition. With your script liner and black paint, go around the outside edges of any petals that seem jagged or blurred. If any white lines still show from your charcoal sketch, lift them away with a damp towel when the surrounding paint is dry. Sign your finished piece and give it a light coat of gloss or semigloss clear acrylic to bring out the colors and protect the finish.

Your finished piece will make a wonderful paperweight or decorative accent.

These are the same rocks featured at the beginning of this chapter.

Impatiens are similar to primroses.

*Painting Flowers on Rocks*

# More Ideas . . .

Many types of flowers can be painted the same as the primroses. By changing the size and shape of individual blossoms, you can come up with countless variations.

An unusual phlox . . .

. . . and a delicate lily of the valley.

*Painting Flowers on Rocks*

# How to Paint
# Tulips

Gazing out at the showy tulips in my spring garden, I've often longed for a way to make them last a little longer. Painting them on rocks is a great way to enjoy their graceful foliage and vividly colored flower heads year round. Their oval blossoms make tulips excellent subjects for beginning painters, and the many colors and kinds should provide even experienced artists with plenty of inspiration. Photographs of flowers are a valuable resource for helping achieve realistic results, so save those flower bulb catalogs!

A number of rock types will work for tulips. A long, narrow fieldstone can be used. Or use a wider fieldstone for an eye-catching stand of tulips. For this demonstration, I selected a river-tumbled rock with an elongated oval shape that tapers to a rounded point. With the addition of a bit of wood filler to level the bottom, it is able to stand alone. If you choose a rock whose base is too uneven or rounded to serve as a stable base, simply "plant" it in a pot and fill in the gaps with kitty litter, gravel, sand, bark mulch or moss.

Once you have picked out a rock, scrub it well to ensure the surface is clean and free of algae, dirt or debris. You may want to experiment by sketching possible layouts before you apply the base coat. This is a good way to explore how to incorporate any natural bumps or bulges into your design. A crack or crease in the surface might be played up as the edge of a curving leaf or a stem, for instance. Turn your rock and examine it from every angle. The highest point is where your topmost blossom should go. Once you've familiarized yourself with your rock, you're ready to begin.

## What You'll Need

- Patio Paint acrylics in Wrought Iron Black, Sprout Green, Dark Eucalyptus Green, Cloud White, Geranium Red and Sunshine Yellow
- assorted brushes, including ¾-inch or 1-inch (19mm or 25mm) square brush, a ¼"inch or ⅜-inch (6mm or 10mm) angle shader, a no. 4 filbert and a no. 0 or 1 script liner
- chalk or white charcoal pencil
- tube of wood filler for leveling the base (optional)

Whether painted as a thick stand or in a small, elegant grouping, rock tulips offer a bit of springtime's best color all year round.

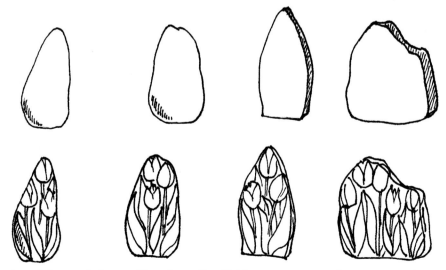

Any of these rock shapes will work as tulips. Height is an important element to consider when selecting a rock.

# 1 Base Coat

Your base coat does not necessarily have to be dark, but the contrast of bright blooms and leaves against a dark background is a most dramatic and striking combination. Use Dark Eucalyptus Green to soften a large puddle of black paint. Cover the entire surface of your rock except the bottom of the base. Allow the paint to dry.

Covering your rock with a black-green base coat provides a dramatic background for the flowers and foliage.

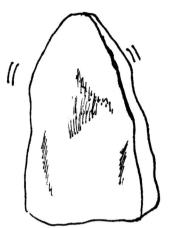

Incorporating bumps, dips and creases into your design will camouflage imperfections and may even add to the realistic look of your creation.

# 2 Layout

Because no two rocks are identical, your own layout may require some adjustment. You'll be painting the whole rock, but start with the side you've selected as your primary focal point. The shape and height of your particular rock will dictate your basic design.

If you plan to set your finished piece into a pot or other container, check the fit now to determine how much rock surface will show. You can vary the height by adding more filler to the pot if needed, so long as you avoid making the piece prone to tipping over. A pot can also serve as a holder while you paint in your flowers.

A classic flower arrangement is the staggered trio, and it can be adapted to a number of rock shapes. Begin with the highest point on the rock and sketch in an oval shape as shown. Depending on the rock, the size of the flower head can vary, but you may want to work close to life size to heighten the illusion of reality. On my rock, which measures nearly 12″ (30.5cm) from top to bottom, the flower heads are about 2½″ (6.4cm) long and not quite 2″ (5.1cm) wide.

Place the second tulip head just below and over to one side of the first. Place the third head slightly lower than the second one, but on the same side as the first. If your rock has room, placing this third flower slightly off center, and not directly below the first, will strengthen your composition. If that isn't possible, try tilting the flower head out toward the edge of the rock just a bit to keep the composition dynamic.

Once you're satisfied with the look of the layout on the primary side, turn your rock to the next blank surface and add one or two flower heads the same size as the first three. Keep turning your rock until you have flower heads at different levels all the way around.

Next, sketch the stems that hold up the flower heads. Some can be straight; others, curved or bowed slightly. Stems for the upper heads may appear to be partially hidden behind lower flowers or leaves.

*Painting Flowers on Rocks*

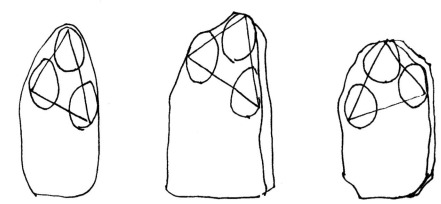

Some variation on a basic triangular design makes for a pleasing composition.

Begin with plain ovals, then give the flower heads volume by curving the petal seams to indicate roundness.

Tulip leaves have a bold, sculptural appearance: narrow at the bottom, fluted out in the center then tapering to a point. Start by sketching full leaves in the largest open spaces first, then fit in others that are partially hidden by flower heads. Allow some to curve upward following the contours of the rock to camouflage the edges. Varying the shape and size of the leaves will avoid an overly regimented look.

Turn your rock as you work, adding leaves or parts of leaves all the way around so only enough of the dark base coat shows for definition and the illusion of depth.

Tulips' shapes change as they open and mature. Use these samples to ensure variety as you detail each flower head.

# 3 Paint the Leaves and Stems

The foliage on many spring flowers—including tulips, narcissus and daffodils—tends to have a bluish green cast. Begin with a small puddle of Dark Eucalyptus Green. Mix in about half as much Sprout Green. Use this color and a medium-sized round brush to fill in the leaf shapes and sturdy stems all the way around.

# 4 Shade the Leaves and Stems

To shadow the foliage, add enough black paint to the green mixture to get a deeper green. Stroke this color down near the edge along the same side of every stem to create the look of roundness. Then run a thicker line of this dark paint along the center of the most dominant leaves, beginning near the base and following the curve of the leaf upward to taper off near the tip. While it's wet, blend it to soften any sharp edges by smudging with your finger, a dry brush or cotton swab. Smaller leaves, and those partially hidden behind flower heads, should have even wider shadows to help make them recede into the background. Also darken around the tops of the stems where the flower heads would naturally cast a shadow.

As you fill in the leaves and stems, look for large spaces of dark base coat that can be minimized by adding more leaves or parts of leaves.

Choose which side will be shaded and paint a thin line along that side of each stem.

Shadow the centers of the leaves, smudging the wet paint to blend away harsh lines.

*Painting Flowers on Rocks*

# 5 Highlight the Leaves and Stems

Begin with the same mixture of greens used for the leaves, brightening it by adding enough Sunshine Yellow to make it stand out against the original green. Use this bright yellow-green and a script liner to outline the leaves in the foreground, particularly along the edges where light would be strongest—that is, along the upper edges—and anywhere the leaves could use more definition. Also, highlight the stems on the side opposite the ones you shadowed. Repeat these details on the stems and leaves all the way around the rock.

# 6 Paint the Tulip Heads

The actual blooms should vary slightly from the simple ovals initially sketched. For some, the two outermost petals remain tightly closed in a teardrop shape. Others are more open with the outer petals clearly defined and interior petals revealed. Use the illustration as a guide to how the simple oval shapes can be individualized, creating a realistic combination of blossoming stages.

Squeeze out a large puddle of Geranium Red, then add just enough Cloud White to soften the red to a bright pink. Apply this with a medium-sized flat or filbert brush. Begin at the rounded bottom of the tulip, drawing your strokes upward to fill in the tops of the petals. Leave narrow traces of your dark base coat showing along the edges of your petal lines to help define them. For solid coverage you may need to apply a second coat after the first dries.

Highlighting helps accentuate stems and leaves.

Smooth, uniformly applied paint is the goal.

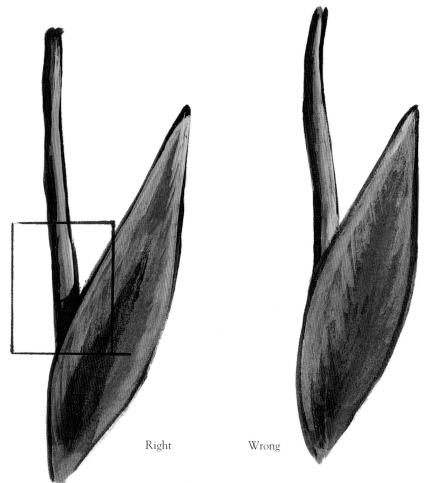

Right          Wrong

Where leaves or stems overlap, use shadows instead of highlights to create depth.

## 7 Shade and Define the Petals

Mix a trace of black into a small amount of straight red paint to produce a deep maroon color. For this next step you can use a slightly smaller filbert brush that is only slightly damp or a round brush that's seen better days, the bristles splaying and somewhat ragged. Feather in this shading color starting with the bottom edge and curving these short strokes slightly to create the illusion of plump contours. On flowers where outer petals meet or overlap, fill in the space below them with shadows. Curve a longer, shadowing line up the center of each full petal to form a subtle spine. Where only a portion of a petal shows, gauge where the center would be and place the curving shadow there. In addition to this spine line, tulip petals have a texture of delicate ridges that can be suggested by drybrushing separated bristles to create more curving lines that angle out and away from the center then upward in gentle curves.

Curving these shading strokes emphasizes the tulips' rounded contours.

## 8 Feather in White Edges

Use a script liner and white paint to add the bold white edges that give these tulips heightened drama. Begin along the topmost edge of the outer petals, gently angling delicate strokes toward the center spine with short, flicking movements. These white strokes should be more dense at the top, becoming shorter and more sparse as you move toward the bottom. Smooth the outside petal edges by running a defining white line around each. Add white edges to whichever parts of the inner petals are showing. Now add a trace of red to your white paint to get a light pink. Begin a second set of gently curving pink lines that slightly overlap the ends of the white ones, extending not quite to the center spine. Detail all the tulips this way.

White edges make the flowers stand out while adding a subtle hint of texture to the petals.

Pale pink lines soften the transition from white to a deeper pink.

Do you see how a simple dark line pulls this tulip bloom forward?

# 9 Finishing Touches

Rinse out your script liner and mix a pink similar to the base color of the tulips. Use it to paint around the bottom edges of all your tulips, setting them off against the background. Another way to help make the tulips stand out cleanly is by using black paint to redefine any place where a tulip head overlaps a leaf or stem.

Look your piece over from every angle to be sure all your flowers, leaves and stems are cleanly and clearly rendered. A light spray of clear acrylic sealer will bring out the colors and protect the surface.

While my rock has a base that allows it to stand alone, I think a pot gives it a more finished look, just as a nice frame dresses up a painting.

Dark outlines help to redefine the stems and leaves, too.

Bold and beautiful, your finished piece can
be displayed alone . . .

. . . or set in a decorative pot.

# More Ideas . . .

The basic tulip design is flexible enough to appeal to both beginning and experienced painters.

Tulips can be simple, as shown in this stylized arrangement.

Combine tulips with other spring flowers to create a colorful, mini-garden in a bowl or planter.

Experienced painters may want to try something more elaborate, like this design copied from an old Dutch master's lush still life.

*Painting Flowers on Rocks*

# How to Paint
# Daisies

With their starched white petals and sunny yellow centers, daisies are delightfully fresh, wholesome subjects that already enjoy wide popularity among artists. Painted rock daisies lend a country air to any setting, whether serving as a centerpiece on a picnic table, brightening a front porch or decorating a set of steps. Best of all, they're both fun and easy to paint.

Thick fieldstones make particularly good daisy rocks. Look for rocks that have tapering ends with squared-off bottoms that resemble pots, and larger, more rounded or angular tops that suggest spreading foliage. Finding these rock shapes may take some practice, but they are surprisingly common. Sometimes turning a rock over and around will help you find the elements you're looking for.

If you have a promising rock but it won't stand alone, try adding Plastic Wood or Real Wood Filler to level the base. Another solution is to find a clay pot that you can set your rock in. Before going on, make sure all surfaces are scrubbed clean.

A bit of wood filler can correct an uneven base.

---

**What You'll Need**

- Patio Paint acrylics in Wrought Iron Black, Cloud White, Sprout Green, Sunshine Yellow, Geranium Red, Patio Brick and Woodland Brown
- assorted brushes, including a ¼-inch (6mm) angle shader, a large flat brush, a medium round brush or filbert and a script liner
- chalk or white charcoal pencil
- wood filler (optional)

---

The rocks on the right are perfect examples of free-standing daisy rocks, but planting a less-than-perfect rock in a real pot works, too.

Here's a sample daisy layout step by step.

# 1 Layout

It may be helpful to make a preliminary sketch on your rock to aid in visualizing how the finished piece might look. For rocks that will stand alone, determine the height of the pot first. It shouldn't take up more than a third of the total surface, since you'll want plenty of space for greenery and flowers. Curving the line that indicates the top rim of the pot will make it appear rounded. Turn your rock, extending this line all the way around at the same height. Place a parallel line about an inch below the first to form the pot's narrow upper cuff.

# 2 Base Coat

A dark background will help set off your plant's details. Use black softened slightly with Sprout Green for a more natural look. A large brush makes for quick coverage as you fill in the entire upper portion of your daisy rock. Leave the pot unpainted for now.

# 3 Sketch the Details

Daisy heads come in a variety of sizes, from delicate "fairy blossoms" to giant, showy hybrids. The diameters of your daisies are up to you, but they will look best if you keep them 2″ to 3″ (5.1cm to 7.6cm) across. The sizes of individual flower heads on the same plant may be different, so don't be too concerned about making them all uniform. Aim for ten to eleven petals per flower head surrounding a round center approximately ½″ (1.3cm) in diameter.

The same rocks with sketched-on designs.

Daisy plants look best when you paint lots of flowers, so sketch on as many as you can fit without crowding out too much of the dark base coat needed to define them. A sharpened white charcoal pencil is better for this than chalk since the petals are delicate. Begin at or near the top of the rock, and, if your rock has enough space on the top, make sure you sketch blossoms there as well. Don't neglect the sides and back. Some flowers should be close enough for sets of petals to touch and even overlap in places. Cluster the bulk of these blossoms in the top half of the plant portion of your rock, leaving space between the top of the pot and the lowest flowers for leaves and stems. Don't hesitate to wash off your sketch marks and start over until you're satisfied.

Darken the upper portion of the rock, leaving about a third or less to serve as the pot.

Complete the layout by running stem lines in varying widths from just above the rim line to connect with the flower heads. Vary the width and angle of the stems, and have a few vanish behind lower flowers, appearing again directly above where they connect to taller blossoms.

Once your design is in place, you're ready to paint!

A small gap between the stem bottoms and the top rim of the pot will add to the appearance of depth.

Vary the angle and size of your leaves. Some should appear to be behind the stems, while others overlap them.

Add the leaves next. Daisy leaves have a somewhat ragged look and tend to angle out from the stems. Fit bits and pieces of leaves among your blossoms as well, since you don't want to have more of the dark background showing than is necessary to set off your details and establish the appearance of depth. Don't forget to add leaves and stems to the sides and back of your piece.

## 4 Paint the Stems and Foliage

Mix Sprout Green with enough Sunshine Yellow to create a light green shade. Use a script liner to paint the stem lines. Next, switch to an angle brush and use the same green to fill in the leaves. The tip and edge of the angle brush will allow you to make dabbing strokes that suggest the long, narrow serrations in the leaves. A second coat may be needed to make the leaves stand out. Add more yellow to your green to brighten it a shade, and use this color to add unrefined veins to one side of each leaf. Change to a long script liner and highlight along one side of each stem with this color as well.

Lighter yellow-green brushstrokes add to the overall ragged look of your leaves.

These highlighting lines help emphasize the stems.

*Painting Flowers on Rocks*

## 5 Paint the Flower Heads

Angle shader brushes are perfect for creating the crisp look of individual daisy petals. Make sure the bristles are thoroughly clean and only slightly damp. Dip the angled edge of the brush into white paint, then lightly press it down to form the first petal. As you paint subsequent petals, turn the brush so each petal is perpendicular to the center circle, like sun rays. Otherwise, you will begin to see a very undaisylike whorl pattern emerge. You can always paint over any petals you don't like, or you can redefine them later.

When all the petals are in place on all sides of your rock, switch to a round brush and straight Sunshine Yellow to fill in the centers. It may take more than one coat for solid coverage, but try to leave a narrow crescent of the dark base color showing around the lower portion of each circle for added emphasis.

Petals are actually pressed on lightly rather than stroked.

Bright yellow centers snap these daisies into focus.

Wrapping some daisy heads around the rock's edges helps minimize the rocky shape.

## 6 Add Shadows and Sharpen Contrasts

Some chalk lines are likely to show from your original layout sketch. These can be picked up with a damp cloth or paper towel. To neaten or reshape any petals, mix Sprout Green deepened with black and use a narrow brush to shave down or otherwise correct any petals that need redefining. Also use this dark green to shadow leaves or stem tops where they run up against a flower head. This helps pull the flowers out by making the foliage appear to recede. Carefully inspect all your flowers for places that need these small but vital touches.

Use deep green paint and your script liner to tidy up or shave down the edges of any petals that should be smoother, and to shadow leaves and stems that come in contact with flower heads.

## 7 Paint the Terra-Cotta Pot

To create the warm, earthy color of terra cotta, start with a good-sized puddle of Sunshine Yellow, then add half as much Patio Brick, mixing the two to get a uniform color. Use a large enough brush to quickly cover the unpainted portion of your piece. For the appearance of a shadow below the overhanging cuff, mix a brushful of Woodland Brown into a small portion of the terra-cotta mixture, and stroke in a narrow curving strip of shadow below the bottom line. Carry this shadow line all the way around the rock. Switch to straight Woodland Brown and a script liner to reemphasize the lower edge of the pot's cuff so it stands out cleanly from every angle.

To highlight the top edge of the pot, lighten your original terra-cotta mixture with white and run this all the way around, again using your script liner.

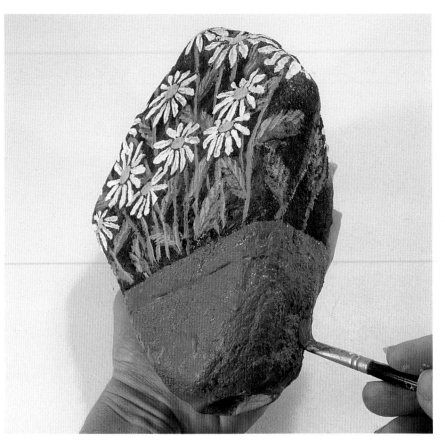

Paint in the terra-cotta pot all the way around the rock.

*Painting Flowers on Rocks*

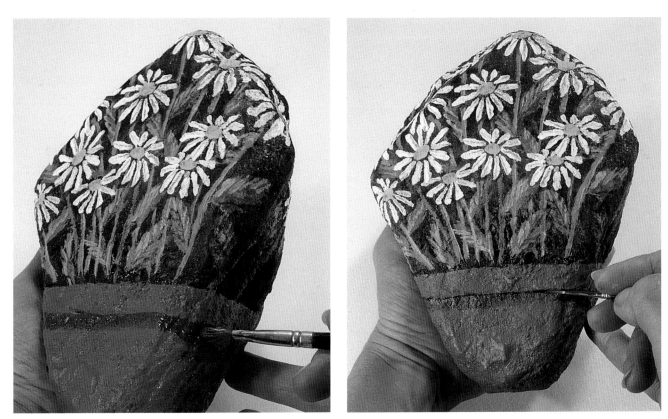

Creating a shadow below the edge of the cuff adds to the illusion of reality.

A dark line further defines the cuff.

Highlighting the rim of the pot.

# 8 Finishing Touches

While you still have that pale terra cotta on your script liner, add a touch of yellow to it and use this soft orange-yellow to create a shallow U-shaped indent in the middle of each yellow daisy center. This is another small detail, but it will add to the realistic look of your daisies.

My rock had a slightly rounded base to begin with, but if your rock base is straight and squared off, you can round the corners by painting them in with a deeper shade of brown. A light coat of clear acrylic spray will enrich your colors.

This small indent in each center adds just the right finishing touch.

Darkening the corners of a square bottom will round them off.

Here are the same three rocks shown at the beginning of this chapter. Wouldn't they look great by your front door?

*Painting Flowers on Rocks*

# More Ideas . . .

Other variations of the daisy design include yellow daisies, black-eyed Susans and sunflowers. You might even want to try multicolored painted daisies in hues that match your decor.

Daisies look terrific displayed outdoors, and if you use weather-resistant paint, your creations should last quite a while. No paint finish is impervious to the long-term effects of weather, but you can lengthen your painted rocks' life spans by keeping them on a covered porch or bringing them in during the harsh winter months.

Create a new look just by changing petal colors.

Van Gogh provided the inspiration for this vase of sunflowers.

Handcrafted with care, this bouquet of black-eyed Susans honors loved ones in a very special way. Painted flowers won't blow away in bad weather or fade like other artificial remembrances do.

*Painting Flowers on Rocks*

# How to Paint
# Hostas

Hosta plants are valued by gardeners for their compact habit, glossy foliage and attractive variations in coloration—the very same characteristics that make them pleasing subjects for rock artists. This flashy, white-edged hosta has emerald-hued leaves trimmed with dramatic slashes of white, which serve to emphasize their simple yet graceful shape. A single large piece or a grouping of several smaller painted plants makes a handsome addition to any interior.

The perfect hosta shape is a half-rounded mound. Hostas look best when painted life size, so search for flat field-stones that stand at least 8″ (20.3cm) tall. Although hosta rocks can be displayed propped against a wall or other surface, a level base that allows the piece to stand alone will make it more versatile. The bigger the rock, the more impressive it will be, so go with the largest rock you feel comfortable tackling. Look for slabs of sedimentary rock that form in layers, making them relatively thin but not too fragile. These are great for painting hostas that look large without being too heavy or hard to handle.

While this rock is not huge, it's a good size for your first project.

Look for a broad, mostly flat base and a tall, rounded top when selecting a hosta rock.

Practice designs can be sketched on using chalk first, then refined further with a marker. Already these rocks are beginning to look more like plants.

Working over the top and around the sides, cover your rock with layers of heart-shaped leaves.

## 1 Layout

Hosta leaves grow in random, overlapping layers of similarly sized leaves. Start by imagining how the leaves might splay fountainlike from the top. Sketch these first, incorporating the top width of the rock. Below this first set, sketch in a slightly larger row of broad, heart-shaped leaves with pointed ends, allowing each one to hang at a slightly different angle. As you work down, only parts of subsequent layers will show; most, but not all, leaves should be overlapped by the leaves above. Allow some leaves to skew sideways or appear foreshortened while others curve around the sides of the rock. Individual leaves should generally point out toward the edges of the rock.

Create visual interest by varying the angles of the leaves and the number of lower leaves that show. By the time you reach the bottom, only pointed leaf tips, in assorted sizes, should be visible. Sketch partial leaves along the top and around the edges to heighten the illusion of a real plant. By using a piece of chalk or a white charcoal pencil for your initial layout, you can erase or adjust various leaves until you have a pleasing and natural looking composition. When you are satisfied with your sketch, go over the leaf outlines with a fine-point marker to make them stand out clearly.

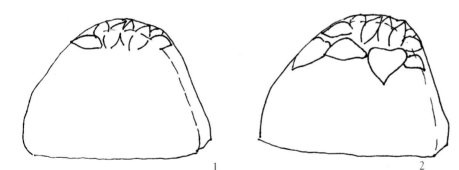

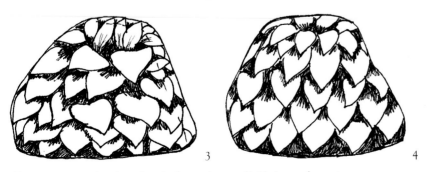

Creating a natural and random look step by step (1-3). It may be easier to create a more structured look (4), which can also make an attractive piece.

*Painting Flowers on Rocks*

## 2 Paint the Voids

Making the areas around the leaves appear to recede gives this hosta the illusion of dimension and helps the leaves stand out. For the strongest possible contrast, use straight black paint beginning along the irregular edge of the bottom leaves.

The size of the brush you use will depend on how large your rock is and how easily you can maneuver in and around the edges of the leaves. On this piece I used a larger flat brush to blacken in the base of the rock and a smaller round brush around the upper leaves. Experiment to determine what brush works best for you. Don't neglect the voids along the sides and top, filling in all the spaces between the leaves. Then paint over the outlines around each leaf to ensure they are well defined.

## 3 Fill In the Leaves

I prefer a ½-inch (13mm) angle shader for painting the base color of the leaves. Use Sprout Green to fill in every leaf shape, being careful not to cover up the black outlines around them. If you do go over any lines, retouch them with black paint when you are finished filling in the green.

The dark shadows between and below the leaves give this piece much of its impact.

Incorporating the rock's top and sides is vital to achieving a realistic and dimensional look.

Begin filling in your leaf shapes along the bottom . . .

. . . and work your way up.

# 4 Add the Veins

Veining lines serve a dual purpose: They emphasize the shape and angle of each individual leaf and also give your leaves the look of subtle highlights if you keep the uppermost portion of each leaf solid green.

Switch to a script liner brush, and add enough Sunshine Yellow to lighten your original green to a bright yellow-green. Mix in a bit of water to ensure that this color flows on smoothly. Too dry and your strokes will clump or break; too wet and the lines will look transparent. Make some test strokes on paper to check the paint's consistency.

Begin with a straight line along the center from the middle to the tip of the leaf. Add slightly inward curving sets of lines along either side of this center one. Allow them to gradually lengthen as you work your way to the outer edges, creating a scalloped look. Continue veining until every leaf is detailed.

Careful veining adds dimension to the whole plant.

Don't neglect the sides and especially the top, which is likely to show when viewed from above.

Painting the veins step by step.

*Painting Flowers on Rocks*

## 5 White Edging

Rinse your script liner brush well and switch to white paint to outline each leaf. First run a solid line around the outside of the leaf, then add a series of short, feathery lines to each side. Repeat on every leaf until the entire rock is detailed.

Crisp white edging really gives this painted plant eye appeal. Note that the feathery lines do not need to be neat or refined.

Touches of black will redefine any areas that look murky.

## 6 Finishing Touches

Switch to black paint and darken the undersides of any leaves that need redefining to help the tips stand out cleanly. Then add enough green to black to create a deep shade that will contrast the plain green of the leaves. Use this to stroke in sets of contrasting vein lines along the uppermost portions of the leaves like shadows, tapering them off between the lighter vein lines below.

Most hostas have long flower spikes that stand out above their foliage, but some have shorter spikes. If you wish to add blooms, paint in two or three narrow stalks that originate in shadowed areas between the leaves about a quarter to a third of the way down from the top of the rock. For the blossoms, use Wild Iris mixed with Dutch Blue. Individual blooms will be small, elongated ovals slanting downward at close intervals along the spikes. Add a touch of white to the blossom color to create highlights along the upper sides, then shadow the lower sides with straight Wild Iris.

Contrasting dark ribs help to emphasize the shadowy tops of the leaves.

The same rocks shown earlier, now transformed.

# More Ideas . . .

Like hostas, poinsettias are constructed entirely of similarly shaped leaves. However, over time the topmost leaves of poinsettias acquire color, making them look more like petals.

*How to Paint a Poinsettia*
Select a rock similar to those used for daisies. Begin by sketching the "flowers" and leaves. As with daisies, the plant-to-pot ratio is about two to one. Start with five-pointed center stars of petals, then add two sets of larger petals in between. Make enough "flowers" to fill much of the rock's surface, then add notched leaves around them. Paint in all the voids with black, and use Metallic Pot O' Gold for a festive container.

Fill in the leaves with Pine Green.

You may need two coats of Geranium Red for good coverage on the "petals."

Mix a bit of black into your red paint and use the resulting burgundy color to shade the petals where they overlap and to indicate their ribbed texture. Darken this burgundy a little more and use a script liner to outline the "petals" so they stand out.

Add Sunshine Yellow to Geranium Red to produce a bright red-orange, and use this to highlight the petal edges and ribs.

Darken Pine Green with black and shade the leaves wherever they touch the flowers. Also use this darker green to indicate diagonal ribs along the leaves.

*Painting Flowers on Rocks*

Add Sunshine Yellow to Pine Green, then use your script liner to outline and highlight the ribs and veins on the leaves.

Add even more yellow, and use this bright yellow-green to create a cluster of dots in the center of each flower.

Lightly scrub in touches of Honest Copper with a dry brush to indicate shadows on the container below the overhanging leaves. Use a few vertical strokes to texture the container sides.

*Painting Flowers on Rocks*

# How to Paint
# Petunias

Does any sight capture the flavor of summer more vividly than a planter spilling over with bright petunias? Add to this appeal a variety of colors and petal conformations, and you have a flower you will never tire of painting. The lush petunias in a neighbor's garden inspired me to select this mix of pastel pinks and purples, all colors made by combining varying amounts of the same three paints: white, Geranium Red and Wild Iris. A rounded blossom shape is one of the simplest, but you may prefer to experiment with petals that range from deeply scalloped to wildly ruffled as well as colors from the most flamboyant of scarlets to boldly striped purples and pinks. Leaves can be simple spearhead shapes or look almost lacy with crimped or serrated edges.

Since petunia petals are thin and quite flimsy, the blossoms tend to fold and droop easily. Collecting photographs that show both flowers and foliage will help you see how to make them look natural from every possible angle.

To capture the impression of a sturdy planter, look for rocks that are squared or rectangular along the bottom half, with a level base that's thick enough to stand alone. Ideally, the upper half should be more irregular and perhaps broader to suggest the spilling over of foliage.

Both jagged fieldstones and rounded river rocks can be used for petunia planters. As with other projects, you can paint this piece any size you like, but it looks best when the planter is fairly substantial. The rock I chose measures just over 6″ (15.2cm) along the bottom, almost 9″ (22.9cm) at its widest point and 7″ (17.8cm) tall at the highest point. It's a couple of inches thick, too, which allows me to wrap the design around the edges and over the top for a more realistic look from every angle.

These petunias inspired my choice of colors.

Both fieldstones and more rounded river rocks can be found in the boxy shapes that make good planters.

# 1 Layout

How high to make the sides of your planter will depend on your taste and the size and shape of your rock. Keep in mind that the flowers are the focal point of the piece. Certainly any planter should not take up more than half the total height. Make it much less than a third, however, and your planter may look like a shallow dish. Use your white charcoal pencil to establish the top edge of the planter, then proceed to fill in the upper portion with round blossom shapes. To look realistic, these flowers should be between 1¾″ and 2½″ (4.4cm and 6.4cm) in diameter. Try to vary your composition so there are places where flowers touch, overlap and flow together, balanced against dark backgrounds which set off the flowers. In addition, while most blossoms can be sketched facing out as circles, foreshorten a few into ovals, or turn them even more to reveal the long, tapering back portion. Don't hesitate to erase your sketch marks and redraw them until you are satisfied with how your overall design looks. Be sure to place a few blooms low enough to overlap the top edge of the planter. You may even add a half-closed fading blossom hanging way down over the side. Sketch a variety of flowers all the way around your rock.

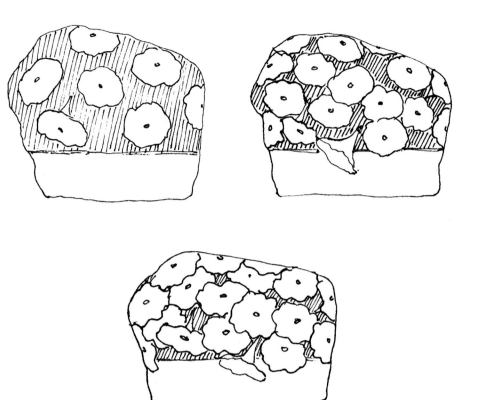

Three examples of possible layouts: the first, too sparse; the second, a pleasing balance; the third, overcrowded.

Here are the two outside rocks with details sketched in black marker.

A white charcoal sketch is easy to erase if you want to make changes.

Four basic petunias from varying angles.

*Painting Flowers on Rocks*

## 2 Base Coat

Use your large square brush to fill in the planter portion with white paint. Paint all sides and the back so the illusion holds from every angle.

Next, mix Sprout Green and black to create a very deep green-black color and use this to fill in the spaces around your flowers. You may need to switch to a smaller brush to fill in the nooks and crannies between and around the blossoms and along the rim of the planter. Another option is to paint the entire top before sketching the flowers, but since petunias have such simple shapes, it is just as easy to paint around them. This also makes it easier to determine if the overall composition of flower and background areas needs adjustment.

Use a large brush for quick coverage. Unless your rock is very pale, you will probably need to apply a second coat.

Painting around the flower shapes is easy because there is little detail involved.

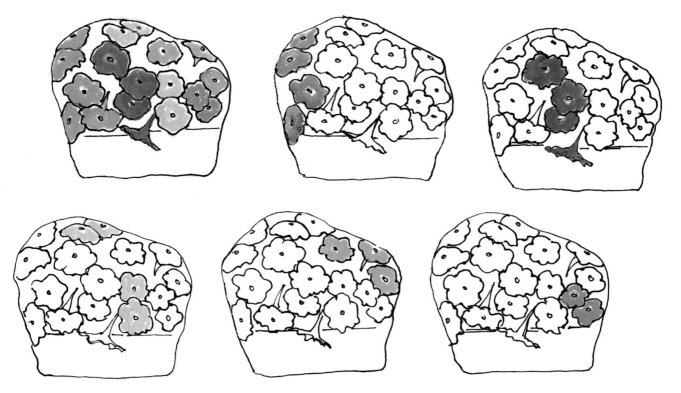

The pattern of color variations broken down into separate steps.

The basic flower shape is round or oval, but you can add individuality with gently undulating outside edges.

## 3 Paint the Flowers

An angle shader brush will help to create crisp petal edges, especially for more ruffled varieties. Begin with a large amount of white and add smaller increments of red until you reach a medium shade of pink (roughly four or five parts white to one part red). Although these petunias are variegated, color groups should be loosely clustered together for a natural look. For your first set, choose either three or five contiguous flower heads and color them all in with the medium shade of pink you just mixed. Leave a small circle unpainted in the center of each blossom.

Turn your rock around and select another group of flowers on the back, perhaps allowing this group to include at least one flower on the side as well. For this next batch of blossoms, begin with the same medium pink and add enough Wild Iris to make a deep purple-pink. The idea is to use colors that relate to one another yet contrast enough to be interesting. Use this new shade to fill in the next set of blooms, choosing a different number to paint—three if you just painted five pinks, for instance.

Rinse your brush and mix a fresh batch of paint, this time using mostly white with just enough red to make a very pale pink. To keep the composition dynamic, fill in two lower flowers with this color, then move to two flowers up near the top of the rock and a few more down the other side.

Now, add a bit more red until the new color falls midway between the two shades of pink already used. Fill in more flowers as you move toward the other end of the piece. Leave just a few remaining front blooms for one additional color variation. Make it by combining the pink you just used with the purple mixed earlier, or add scant brushfuls of Wild Iris to this pink until you have a new color for the remaining flowers.

# 4 Detail the Flower Heads

Just as there are subtle color variations among the flowers, each set of blossoms requires slightly different detailing. For the brightest pink flowers, mix a small amount of red softened with a touch of Wild Iris. Still leaving the center circle unpainted, use a script liner to draw narrow spokelike lines that curve slightly, giving the flower head a soft, convex look.

To detail the deepest purple flowers, darken Wild Iris with a tiny amount of black to make a deep shade that contrasts with the petal color. Besides the curving spokelike lines radiating from the center, add more random short, feathery strokes to emphasize the depth surrounding the center. This deeper shade will also help define the outer edges of the purple petals anyplace they touch or overlap other blossoms. When softened with white, you have a new shade for adding the same kinds of detailing lines and accents to the paler purple blossoms. The palest pink flowers can be detailed with a bright pink.

To fill in the unpainted centers, start with a tiny drop of yellow then add a scant trace of green to make a bright chartreuse and dab this into all the middles. Adding a drop of black to this light green to create a deep gray-green, make a wide, inverted V inside all the centers to create depth.

Note how curving these detailing lines adds depth and dimension to the flower heads.

Though it's a small touch, this simple inverted V-shaped shadow gives each chartreuse flower center some depth and complexity.

These pale highlights can be applied with a fairly large brush as long as you are careful not to paint over the fine detailing lines.

On these deeper pink blooms, the highlighting color is a medium to light pink.

Instead of highlighting the darkest purple flowers, do the reverse. By deepening the shadows along the bottom edge and inside the upper center, the original color will appear to be highlighted.

## 5 Highlight and Shadow the Petals

To give the upper edges and center portions of the palest pink flowers the subtle glow of reflected light, gently scrub a small amount of pigment onto the surface with a dry brush to create soft white streaks that curve between the darker spokelike lines. Extend this lighter color from just above where fine lines shade the centers all the way to the upper reaches of the top petals. Along the lower half of each petal, highlight a smaller section beginning where the short center lines stop and extend a little more than halfway across the petals. For the medium pink flowers, switch to a light pink shade and make your highlights the same way.

The purple flowers, however, will lose some of their impact if you lighten the petals. Instead, mix more of the deep purple used to detail the petals earlier and, again, apply this with a dry brush, adding soft, feathery strokes to both the lower outside edges and upper inside portions of the darker purple flowers. Slightly lighten this color by adding a small amount of white before shading the medium purple flowers.

To create yet another variation, use the palest pink to lighten the centers of the remaining set of pink flowers, stroking it in with a script liner. This pale color can also delineate the outer edge of a turned blossom so it will stand out from the tapering back portion. Use it sparingly to highlight the edges of any purple flowers that need emphasis or more definition.

Before going on, look over your flowers for areas that require this kind of fine-tuning. Anywhere one flower overlaps another, add shadows using the same contrasting detailing colors.

*Painting Flowers on Rocks*

For variety, give some of your flowers pale centers.

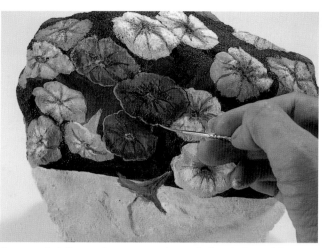

Separate dark flowers from one another with thin, light pink lines . . .

. . . while using deep purple lines to divide and accentuate the lighter-colored flowers.

See how just an edge of deeper-colored shadow pulls one flower out and pushes the other back?

# 6 Paint the Leaves

Mix Sprout Green with a smaller amount of Sunshine Yellow to create an intense green shade. Use a no. 1 or 2 round brush to make the almost abstract-looking leaves and stems. Fit them into all the dark spaces between the flowers, leaving a narrow margin of dark base coat as a buffer wherever leaf and flower meet. Allow some leaves to appear to hang over the white planter. Remember to fill in leaves all the way around the rock.

Darken your original leaf color with a small amount of black. Use this color to shadow your leaf shapes, particularly those areas directly below flowers.

Create these ragged leaves by pressing the tip of a small round brush in short, almost random strokes. Add stems and star-shaped features where the pointed backs of any flowers show.

Touches of a slightly darker green add dimension and subtle contrasts to the foliage.

*Painting Flowers on Rocks*

# 7 Planter Details

Center a long rectangle at the bottom of the planter, on both front and back sides. Paint this space with solid black, making it appear to be an empty space between the short legs of the planter.

Pencil in a simple scalloped edge below the rim. Mix black and white to produce a deep gray, and use your small round brush to paint a shadow along this decorative trim. Switch to a script liner and black paint to make a narrow, defining line along the top edge of the gray scallops.

Use a straightedge, if needed, to help make this long, narrow shape along the bottom of your planter.

Painting the space black seems to make the rock surface disappear.

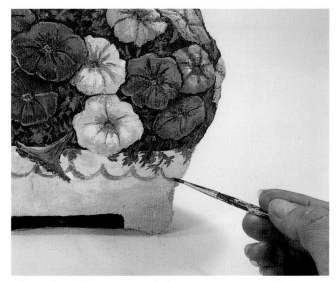

This scalloped design is a simple but attractive way to add character to a plain planter.

A thin black line brings the scallops into focus.

## 8 Finishing Touches

Mix a slightly lighter shade of gray than the one used to shadow the scallops, and create the appearance of more shadows cast on the planter by overhanging flowers and leaves. With straight white paint, go back to accentuate the curved edge of each scallop, avoiding those areas that are shadowed.

Examine your piece from every angle, looking for areas that need more detail. When you are satisfied, spray your petunias with a light coat of acrylic sealer to brighten and protect the colors.

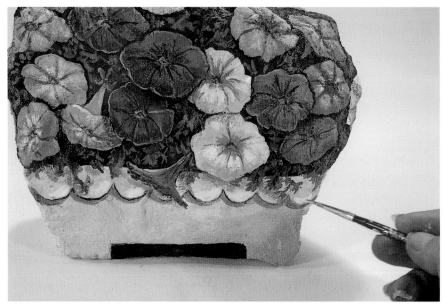

White highlights sharpen the impact of the scallops.

Small shadows really add to the illusion that the flowers and leaves are standing out.

A finished planter of petunias, ready to brighten a whole room.

*Painting Flowers on Rocks*

# More Ideas . . .

Planters are available in many different designs and types, including terracotta and wooden lattice.

Petunias look wonderful in large groupings, so try your hand at some other color combinations and fill a windowsill, deck or maybe your whole yard with color!

Dress up a kitchen table . . .

. . . a walkway . . .

. . . or a front porch with painted rock flowers.

*Painting Flowers on Rocks*

# How to Paint
# Daffodils

Sunny yellow daffodils are a welcome sign of spring's arrival, but, like tulips, they fade away much too soon. Painting them on rocks is a great way to capture their dramatic beauty to enjoy year-round.

There are many ways to approach daffodil and narcissus rocks. If you have access to river-tumbled rocks, select a long, oval-shaped one with a flat end to serve as the base. Or, you might choose a fieldstone with a long narrow or fluted shape suggestive of a clump of flowers. You can use wood filler to level a slightly uneven base, or you might try setting the rock in a planter or vase. The most important feature is that the rock be tall enough to convey the graceful height of these flowers.

Both river rocks and fieldstones can be used for daffodils. The most important element is the height of the rock.

## What You'll Need

- Patio Paint acrylics in Wrought Iron Black, Cloud White, Sunshine Yellow, Geranium Red, Dark Eucalyptus Green and Sprout Green
- assorted brushes, including a large square brush, small and medium round brushes, filberts or angle shader brushes and a long script liner
- chalk or white charcoal pencil
- small decorative planter (optional)
- wood filler (optional)

An uneven base can be built up using wood filler or you can simply plant your daffodil rock in a pot.

# 1 Base Coat

As with most projects in this book, a dark base is the most effective way to create attractive contrasts. Start with a generous puddle of black paint softened slightly with Dark Eucalyptus Green. Use a large square brush to cover the entire upper portion of the rock, including the top and the sides all the way around.

# 2 Layout

Begin by deciding how big you want your flower heads to be. Their size determines how many flowers will fit on your rock, and larger flowers pack more visual punch. A 2½" to 3" (6.4cm to 7.6cm) span is about right for the 9" (22.9cm) tall rock I chose.

On a rounded river rock, flowers can easily be painted around the curved sides. Working on a stone with more defined edges, however, it's better to contain blooms to individual sides—trying to wrap them around corners tends to look odd. An exception is around the top of the rock in front, where having flowers span both surfaces can help disguise an abrupt angle. Work with the unique shape of your particular rock, tailoring your composition to fit any angles or bulges. Keeping your flowers in the upper half of the plant portion of your piece will help give the greenery its characteristic height.

Place your first flower so the top three petals fit into the highest point on the side you've selected as the front of the piece. It is helpful to have a photograph of daffodils as you sketch to see how the heads tilt in different directions. Some petals will also touch or overlap to give your composition more interest. Don't hesitate to erase your sketch with a damp cloth and start over until you are happy with the way it looks.

Flower heads are made up of two basic parts: (1) a star, formed by six outer petals, and (2) the trumpet-shaped center cup, which extends outward and ends with a ruffled rim. Sketch all the outer petals first, then add the centers. Some centers should tilt slightly sideways while others angle down, and keep one or two centers exactly in the middle as though facing straight out. Place one flower mainly on the top surface, but with the lower petals extending down into the front side. Similarly, have another blossom primarily on the front side, but with its upper petals extending to integrate the top angle of the rock.

Apply a dark base coat to the entire rock, leaving only the bottom unpainted—that's where you'll sign the finished piece.

Let the shape of your rock guide your design, incorporating any bumps or bulges. Leave lots of room for long stems and leaves.

*Painting Flowers on Rocks*

Daffodils have tall, narrow stems and long, slightly wider leaves which sprout up alongside the stems. Make sure you extend stems to the upper flowers, and fill in areas around and between flowers with leaves so a minimum of the dark base coat shows.

Usually, trying to bend flowers around sharp angles isn't a good idea, except along the tops, where flowers can span and integrate the two angles.

Use long, smooth strokes to create the graceful foliage.

Note how varying the widths of these highlighting lines gives them a more natural look.

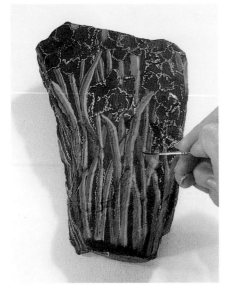

Keep a narrow margin of bright green showing along the edge you're shading. These shadowing lines don't need to be uniform and may even look feathered or smudgy in places.

It's a small touch, but darkening the tops of your stems and leaves where they are directly beneath flower heads will help add dimension.

# 3 Paint the Foliage

Begin with a small puddle of Dark Eucalyptus Green, then mix in about half as much Sprout Green. Use a medium-sized round or filbert brush to fill in the stems and leaves all the way around your rock. Switch to a smaller brush and add a drop of white to a portion of your green mixture. Use this lighter shade of green to create a narrow highlighting line along the right side of every stem and wider lines along the right side of every leaf.

Create the appearance of shadow by darkening the original green mixed for the foliage with a bit of black and stroking it in a narrow line next to, but not on, the edges of the opposite sides of each stem and leaf. Also, shadow the upper ends of the stems and leaves where they meet the sketched flower heads. Shadow the lower edge of any leaf where it's overlapped by another as well. These darker shading lines can also help tidy up any rough edges on leaves and stems. Don't worry about traces of chalk that may still show. When your paint is dry, these marks can be lifted with a damp cloth.

# 4 Paint the Flower Heads

Pour out a tablespoonful of Sunshine Yellow, then add small amounts of black and mix until you get a grayed value that's about 50 percent darker than plain yellow. Use a medium-sized round or angle shader brush to fill in all the outer petals and the portions of the outer trumpet shapes that show, leaving the rounded interior circle unpainted for now. Work all the way around the rock until every flower head is filled in this way. Now add enough black paint to darken this gray-yellow a shade more, and use this mixture on your smallest brush to create shadows below the center cup.

Petals and centers shown facing straight out, slightly tilted, sideways and pointed down.

Switch to straight Sunshine Yellow. Use whichever brush feels most comfortable to begin outlining the petals, then stroke in toward the centers, careful to leave traces of the base coat showing where the petals meet, and varying amounts around and especially beneath the center cups as well.

Use the tip of your smallest tapered brush to dab on the ruffled edge that decorates each trumpet-shaped center. To fill in the inside of the trumpet, mix a trace of Geranium Red into a small amount of Sunshine Yellow to make a soft orange. Leave a rough crescent of the dark undercoating showing along the upper edge to suggest depth, and traces where the orange center meets the yellow ruffled edge, for added definition. Deepen a portion of this orange with a bit more red and feather in a hint of shadowing along the upper edge of the center cup.

A gray-yellow base coat helps subsequent layers of paint stand out against the dark background.

These simple half circles offer a side glimpse of the trumpet-shaped center cups.

Although much of this shading will be covered up, it helps emphasize the dramatic shape of these flowers.

Bright yellow brushstrokes bring these flowers to life. Note that the petals remain distinct from one another while soft edges and traces of shading remain.

Filling the centers with a contrasting pale orange creates depth and visual interest.

A slightly deeper orange shadows the center inside and upper edge.

# 5 Flower Head Details

Using a script liner brush, add small touches of sunny orange to give the petals a look of subtle ridges, particularly on the shadowed sides. Other areas to target for touches of orange include the seams where the petals attach to the trumpets and any places where the outside ruffles could use a bit of definition.

Use a long script liner brush to take up a tipful of plain Sunshine Yellow and place a tapered, beaklike stamen along the top of each center cup, pointing in the same direction the cup is angled if the flower is turned. Note that the base of the stamen doesn't quite touch the ruffle, leaving a dark edge in place to keep each element distinct. While you have yellow on your brush, carefully add some short lines radiating out along the bottom inside of each trumpet's interior to suggest a pleated texture.

Subtle touches of soft orange act like a warm blush upon the petals.

Always make the stamen appear to peek out from the upper edge.

These narrow accenting lines add texture to the center cup.

# 6 Finishing Touches

Mix black and yellow to create a dark, warm gray. Use this on the tip of your script liner to redefine the jutting shapes of the center trumpets anywhere the shape needs to be more distinct.

Dampen your brush to dilute this paint to a transparent tint, and stroke in fine lines like subtle ribs in the lower sets of petals. Switch to black with a touch of green and paint around the tips of any petals that need to be pulled out from their surrounding foliage.

To brighten the overall color of the flowers, mix a bit of white into Sunshine Yellow to soften it and brush on highlighting smudges along the middles and tips of the upper sets of petals to create a subtle glow.

Additional detailing touches help to clarify shapes . . .

. . . and create the look of subtle ridges across the lower petals.

A final splash of pale yellow highlights the upper petals.

*Painting Flowers on Rocks*

# More Ideas . . .

According to my collection of flower catalogs, the variations possible with daffodils and narcissus are nearly infinite. Try some small, delicate paper whites, for instance, or one of the many combinations of petal and cup colors. Displaying your finished flowers in different containers will change their look, as well.

Here is another color combination I found in a gardening catalog.

Narcissus are a more simple and delicate variation you may want to try.

Whether single or in small groups, these painted pieces make an eye-catching display.

Painting Flowers on Rocks

# How to Paint
# Caladiums

An extravagance of brightly colored speckles and lavish splashes make caladium leaves the rival of any flower for showy display. Their sensational good looks mask a surprising fact: Caladiums are actually quite easy to paint. The only hard part is choosing from among the dazzling variety of color combinations. Even the relatively sedate white caladium with plain green veining makes an appealing subject. Caladium rocks look particularly nice when displayed in pots and planters. For this project, I couldn't resist an over-the-top combination of reds, pinks and greens that only Mother Nature could have dreamed up.

Flat fieldstones in odd, irregular shapes make the best upright caladiums. You might find a rock that is wide rather than tall, with uneven contours that suggest the look of a sprawling stand of caladium leaves. Rocks with flat bases that allow them to stand alone are fine, but since I often come across broken pieces while rock hunting, here is an opportunity to show how to make good use of them. Pointed angles lend themselves to being planted in pots or flower beds.

Real caladium leaves can be quite petite (under 2″ [5.1cm] across) or bigger than a dinner plate. Plan on painting leaves that are at least 3″ (7.6cm) across and 4″ to 5″ (10.2cm to 12.7cm) long. The rock you choose should be large enough to fit at least half a dozen full and partial leaves onto the front or primary side. Thin rocks can be used; arrange them in layers with others to heighten the illusion of dimen-

sion. While the rock's surface should be smooth enough to allow for fine detailing, it certainly doesn't need to be uniformly flat; curves, dips and creases can actually enhance your design. Make sure the rock you choose is scrubbed clean before going on.

## What You'll Need

- Patio Paint acrylics in Wrought Iron Black, Woodland Brown, Sprout Green, Cloud White and Geranium Red
- assorted brushes, including a no. 0 or 1 script liner and a medium flat brush
- chalk or white charcoal pencil
- black fine-point marker (optional)
- the corner cut from a regular (used, if possible) kitchen sponge

As colorful as they are, these live caladiums do not include some of the most spectacular varieties.

Broken pieces of rocks can be set in pots. Match rock and container before painting to ensure a good fit.

As you can see, the design for these pieces is really quite simple.

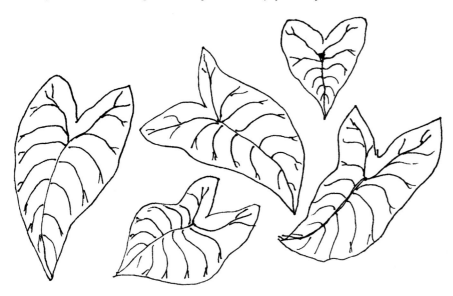

Here's an assortment of leaf shapes and angles to help your composition achieve a realistic look.

# 1 Layout

The basic leaf shape is that of an elongated, somewhat misshapen heart. Each leaf grows on a single thin stalk, often tilting one way or another, but with the tapering end generally pointing downward.

Start at the upper edge of the rock face selected as the front, and sketch your first set of full leaves. Working down from there, fit partial leaves below the first set. Have some of your leaves tilt in or out, while others point straight down to avoid a composition that's too rigid or predictable. My rock is several inches wide across the top, providing just enough room to fit a narrow leaf or two before turning the rock to sketch side and rear leaves. Avoid leaving too many large spaces between your leaves.

Doing your preliminary sketch in charcoal or chalk allows you to adjust your design or even wash it away and start over. When you're satisfied, it may be helpful to trace over your chalk lines with a fine-point marker to make them stand out.

My choice is a misshapen triangle of rock. The tapering end will fit easily into a pot.

Allow the shape of your rock to suggest the placement of leaves. While you should avoid leaving large voids between leaves, small voids are desirable to set off and define individual leaf shapes.

Going over the design with a dark marker will help you to see the composition more clearly.

## 2 Paint the Voids

Dark areas appear to recede into the background, so painting the voids between leaves is a simple way to make unwanted surfaces seem to disappear. Use any brush large enough to fill in these areas quickly yet neatly with a mixture of Woodland Brown and black. Allow this paint to dry before going on.

Use a brown-black mixture and a medium brush to fill in the voids all around the rock.

Paint all your leaves solid green, taking care to keep the edges smooth.

Cover your marker lines with paint.

### 3 Paint the Leaf Base Coat

Pour out a good-sized puddle of Sprout Green and fill in all the leaves on your rock. You may need to use a smaller brush to fill in the tapering leaf ends. When the green paint is dry, switch to straight black and use your script liner to outline each leaf, covering the marker lines.

### 4 Establish Shadows

Mix enough black into your green paint to produce a dark green. Apply this deep green to any area that would naturally appear to be shadowed; this includes margins where top leaves overlap lower ones. Keep your brush on the dry side so these shadowed areas can be scrubbed in or blended rather than leaving noticeable lines. Create these softly shadowed areas all around your piece.

The top leaves need little or no shadowing; those below should be shaded wherever leaves overlap.

## 5 Add Highlights

The purpose of highlighting is to enhance the illusion that the leaves have curved surfaces and a slightly ribbed texture. Mix enough white into your green paint to lighten it to a discernibly paler shade of green. An old, ragged brush is ideal for this, as frayed bristles tend to separate, making several lines with every stroke. You may also use a narrower brush and stroke in individual highlights. Note that the bulk of these lines are concentrated on the right sides of the leaves, creating the illusion that the strongest light source is coming from that direction. Note, too, that these lines are quite substantial as I want them to show up even under the speckles to follow.

## 6 Speckling

It would be time consuming, and perhaps impossible, to create a realistically random speckled effect by painting in hundreds of individual dots. Instead, clip a small corner off a kitchen sponge and moisten it so it is damp but not dripping. Place a drop of red and a drop of white side by side on your paint dish, and swirl the two colors together with the wrong end of your paintbrush so they intermingle rather than blend together. Choosing the side with the most texture, dip the sponge lightly into the swirled paint. Make a few practice speckles on newsprint to check the color and consistency, and to remove any excess paint. Press the sponge down gently and lift it straight up to avoid smudging. Now you are ready to speckle your first leaf.

Start with the leaves on the back or side of your rock. This allows you to refine your technique before moving on to the primary side. Don't try to make each leaf look exactly the same. Instead, deliberately vary the direction in which you apply the sponge to the surface and the way you pick up paint from your palette, to create variations in both the amount of speckles and their placement. The

Short curving lines of varying widths along the leaves' edges create the appearance of reflected light.

speckles should be concentrated in a Y shape that reflects the underlying framework of the leaf, with indistinct lines of speckles along the ribs. Sprinkle a few at the edges, too. Remember that you can always paint out any speckles with Sprout Green and redo them if needed. Let these dry.

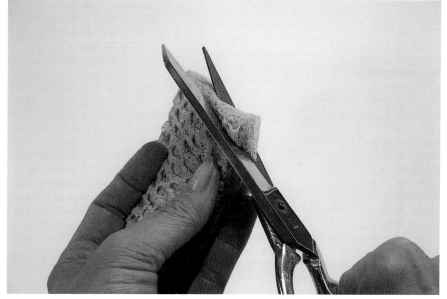

The corner of an ordinary kitchen sponge provides all the texture needed to make convincing speckles.

Note how this loose pattern of speckles creates a subtle Y shape that echoes the veining to follow.

# 7 Add the Veining

The narrow lines of the veins and spine are the real focal point of the leaves. Apply them with your script liner brush and Geranium Red paint. You may need to adjust the consistency of your paint by adding a small amount of water. Veining strokes should flow smoothly, without clumping or breaking, but the pigment should not be so watery that the veins seem transparent. Make the main Y shape first, then branch curving lines off the center spine, allowing them to taper off just before you reach the outer leaf edges. As with speckling, it's wise to start with the back leaves first for practice, then work your way around to the front.

# 8 Finishing Touches

Once all the leaves are speckled and veined, go back around the outsides of any leaves that need redefining, especially if there are any stray speckles. Rinse your brush and mix a bit of the same pale green used earlier for highlighting. Run very narrow outlines around the outside leaf edges to help them stand out from the background.

Now look your caladium over from every angle to make sure all the leaves are well defined and detailed. A light coat of acrylic spray will protect the surface and add depth to the colors.

The main Y shape of the veining should relate to the actual shape of the leaf. Make some look more or less straight and others wavy, crooked or bowed.

Go over any black outline that may have been obscured by speckles.

These light outlines don't need to be too consistent. Leave a few plain places and vary the width of the lines, too.

# More Ideas . . .

Painted rock caladiums add riveting color and texture to any setting. Dress up a set of steps or use them to fill in that bare spot in your garden. Indoors, display them in a planter or ceramic container. Caladiums are so much fun to paint that once you've tried one variety, you'll want to try others!

Real and painted plants complement one another while brightening up an off-season flower bed.

Use rock caladiums to dress up a set of steps . . .

. . . or group them in a clay pot for a colorful outdoor display.

*Painting Flowers on Rocks*

# How to Paint
# Pansies

When these happy-faced flowers bob merrily in spring and fall flower beds, it's almost impossible to keep from smiling back. Although pansies come in an array of solid colors, it's the distinctive facelike markings and startling combinations of whites, blues, yellows and burgundies that attract my artist's eye. Those very same elements are what make them a fun, if slightly more challenging, subject for rock painters. Being able to enjoy the look of these whimsical blooms anytime and anywhere makes learning to paint them well worth the effort.

Almost any size and shape of rock may be used to create a clump of pansies. I've selected three different rock types that will work: a broken piece of fieldstone, a rounded river rock and a chunky rock picked up along the side of a rural road. Avoid rocks with overly rough surfaces and those with lots of creases or other features that will make it difficult to paint lines and details.

With preliminary flowers and foliage sketched on, it's easy to see how each type of rock can be transformed. For the first two, I opted to incorporate contain-ers into the composition, while the third and smallest is designed to fit in a shallow terra-cotta dish. If you choose to display your pansy this way, matching your rock to its planter before painting ensures a good fit. It may be helpful to sketch a practice design even though it will be covered over when you paint the base coat. This exercise will give you a feel for the unique contours and possible challenges each rock presents. It will also allow you to establish the best place for the top edge of the container if you plan to include one.

## What You'll Need

- Patio Paint acrylics in Wrought Iron Black, Cloud White, Sprout Green and Sunshine Yellow
- Apple Barrel acrylics in Dutch Blue and Wild Iris
- Metallic FolkArt Artist's Color (by Plaid) in Pearl White
- assorted brushes, including a medium to large flat brush, angle brushes in ⅜-inch and ⅛-inch (10mm and 3mm), a no. 4 or 6 round brush and a no. 0 or 1 script liner
- chalk or white charcoal pencil

While each of these rocks is a different type, they all have a flat base and compact shape.

Practice sketches like these will help you see how your rock will work.

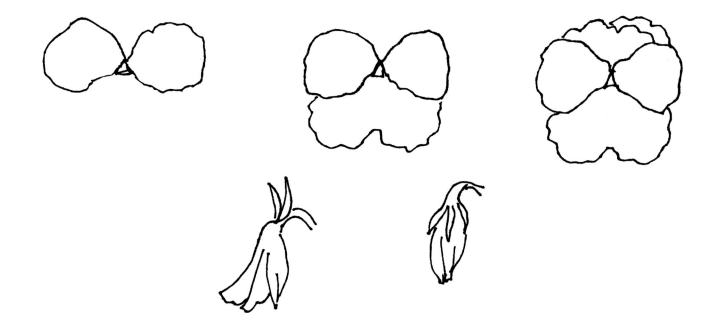

Common blossom and bud shapes.

### 1 Base Coat

Mix Sprout Green and black to produce a very deep black-green shade. Use a large brush to quickly cover the entire upper surface of your rock (or the whole rock if you are not including a container). When the top has dried, paint your container. I'm using Sunshine Yellow that will be toned down later.

### 2 Layout

The basic conformation of pansy blossoms begins with two separate middle petals spread out like little wings, a conjoined set below and two overlapping, half-round petals above. Use a white charcoal pencil and aim to cover approximately 60 percent of the plant portion of the rock. While hybrid pansy varieties can be as big as 4″ (10.2cm) across, the average size is 2″ to 3″ (5.1cm to 7.6cm) as measured across the middle petals. Your individual rock will dictate how you lay out your overall design. Try to place some blooms quite close to each other, even partially overlapping, while others stand alone.

Cover the upper portion with a dark base coat. Note that the height of the container is quite low, leaving more room for flowers.

Have at least one flower droop over the container edge and incorporate one or two buds and perhaps one fading bloom or side view. This variety will add to the visual interest of your creation. Fill in the spaces between the flowers with long, oval leaves whose edges are gently scalloped. Use whole leaves in larger spaces and partial leaves, either tips or edges, in smaller spaces. Allow three or four leaves on each side to hang over the edge of your painted container.

*Painting Flowers on Rocks*

Sketch a similar design on the back of the rock and fill in the sides as well. Once you are satisfied that your pansies are neither too sparse nor too crowded, you are ready to begin painting.

A sample composition. Note how blossoms tilt in various directions for a more natural, less structured look.

It may take two coats to get solid coverage of light colors.

A sharpened charcoal pencil is ideal for sketching in the details of your flowers and leaves.

Leave narrow edges of the dark base coat showing between the petals for definition. If you accidentally cover any portion of these spaces, go back over them with a script liner and dark paint.

These little white apron shapes don't need to be identical, as it is desirable to have slight variations among your flowers.

Touches of Wild Iris should be stroked on lightly.

## 3 Paint the Flower Shapes

Mix a small amount of Dutch Blue into a larger puddle of white to create a hazy pastel blue. Use a ⅜-inch (10mm) angle shader to fill in the petal shapes, leaving narrow edges of base coat showing between the individual petals to keep them distinct. It may take more than one coat to make this petal color stand out.

## 4 Flower Details

By the time you've filled in all your petal shapes, the first ones should be dry. Use a ⅛-inch (3mm) angle brush and plain white paint. Stroke in two small wing shapes inside the two full middle petals, then sweep down from the flower center into the lower petals to create an apronlike shape that takes up nearly the whole midsection of these lower petals. This white detailing will not be visible on any unfurled buds or fading blooms.

Next, switch to a small round brush or filbert. A ragged one with separating bristles is ideal for the next step. Lightly drybrush straight Wild Iris outward from the edges of the white aprons you just painted. These strokes should just slightly overlap the white before feathering out into the middles of the petals, resembling delicate veins. Stop your strokes short of the edges of the petals, leaving at least a third of the blue base color uncovered. Add spare strokes of this color to your buds, lightly feathering up from the bottom. Use it to detail any drooping flowers, too, suggesting shadowed folds along the length.

Mix Wild Iris with enough black to produce a burgundy so deep that it is only a shade or two short of black. Use your smallest angle brush or small round brush to create dark patches on either side of the two middle petals. Leave a rim of white showing around the top and sides, but along the bottom allow

*Painting Flowers on Rocks*

this deep purple to go right to the petal's edge. On the conjoined bottom petals, make an even larger dark patch that covers all but the sides and top of the white apron shape with perhaps a trace of white showing along the bottom where the patch feathers out into it.

To detail the partial petals at the top, mix a touch of black into a small amount of Dutch Blue and add a scant brush tip full of water to keep the texture loose. Use a script liner brush to shadow the area where the petals meet, stroking a few delicate lines upward to fan into the midsection of the dominant petal. Accentuate the contours of the second, mostly overlapped upper petal, too. Add more of these blue shadows and veins sparingly to the lower portions of the center petals on a few of your flowers just for variety. In addition, add a few touches of this blue-gray to any buds or wilting blossoms for added definition and shading.

Still using a script liner brush, switch to plain white paint and begin highlighting the upper edges of the petals, first outlining the wavy tops, then adding tiny, splinterlike lines to suggest these petals are pleated as well as slightly ruffled. Lightly run a broken line of white to accent the bottom edges of the lower petals as well. If needed, add to the white edges on either side of the dark apron center to make this element more distinct. A few pale highlighting strokes along the tops of any fading blooms and buds will complete them.

Blue-gray shadows add that important element of dimension to your pansies . . .

Note how these patches are set off by the remaining edges of white.

. . . especially when paired with contrasting highlights. Narrow lines of white emphasize how thin the petals are.

# 5 Paint the Foliage

Use straight Sprout Green and your smallest angle brush to begin filling in the leaf shapes, always leaving dark margins of base coat showing around the flowers to keep them distinct. Paint in the whole leaves first, along with the stems supporting any buds. Once these are in place, add partial leaves at various angles and in various sizes until there are no large areas of the dark base showing. You may need to do more than one coat to completely cover this darker paint. Place a couple of pointed features like a pair of rabbit's ears atop any wilting blooms. On folded buds, these little ears should droop down to enclose the top of the bud.

Next, mix enough black into your original green paint to reach a green color that falls between the dark underlying base coat and the color of the leaves. Use this to add a center crease line to all the leaves and to add shadows to the leaves anywhere they are overlapped or overhung by flowers. This will make the leaves appear to recede, in turn helping the flowers stand out. Add a few sets of narrow vein lines to the leaves here and there, giving them a bit of texture.

To highlight the leaves, begin with Sprout Green and add just enough Sunshine Yellow to brighten the green to a lighter shade. Again, use your small angle brush to create a series of gentle scallops along the edges of the leaves. Add a narrow highlighting line right alongside the darker center crease line and scatter small sets of vein lines opposite the darker ones painted earlier. Concentrate these highlights on more

When filling in leaf and stem shapes, remember that leaving traces of dark undercoating helps give your flowers a realistic appearance.

Shade the portions of leaves that adjoin any flower head. Note how I left narrow outlines of dark paint around all my flower heads to keep them distinct.

*Painting Flowers on Rocks*

exposed or full leaves, highlighting fewer partial and overlapped leaves.

To add emphasis to leaves hanging over the edge of your container, outline them with the dark green, especially along the lower edges. Create the illusion of shadow along the container by mixing a small amount of Sunshine Yellow with an even smaller amount of black to produce a soft yellow-gray. Make a series of smudged shadows along the same side with overhanging leaves and blossoms.

Lighter green highlights add texture and definition to leaves.

Although it's a small touch, these gray shadows lift the flowers and leaves away from the bowl, adding to the illusion of depth.

## 6 Detail the Container

While your particular container may be any color you prefer, one way to create the soft iridescent finish of some ceramic glazes is to overcoat the original color with a pearlized paint. I used FolkArt paint in Pearl White to tone down my yellow so it wouldn't compete with my pansies. Avoid painting over your shadows. Highlight the lip of the bowl with more Pearl White. A simple, narrow trim line of deep blue around the lip will help to define the bowl. If you are painting on a rounded rock, it will be naturally shadowed around the bottom. On flat fieldstones, add the look of rounded contours by mixing more of the yellow-gray used to shadow under the leaves, and add some softly curved shadows along the very bottom of the container.

A light coat of Pearl White acts like a glaze to give my bowl the look of ceramic glaze. Add a second coat to the rim's edge to make it stand out.

You can detail your bowl with a simple line of trim or try something fancier.

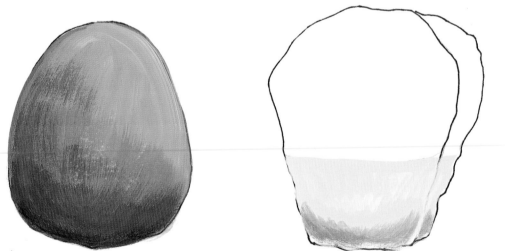

Curving lines of smudged shadow round out a flat rock's surface.

# 7 Finishing Touches

To complete your pansy faces, use the tip of your liner brush to tuck a tiny Sunshine Yellow "nose" into each flower's center at the point where the deep purple patch meets the white triangle that marks the top of the lower petals. Next, turn your rock slowly around, looking for places that need more definition, such as more dark outlines or more shadowing.

Use cheery pansy rocks to fill planters and window boxes. Inside, they look especially pretty on kitchen windowsills or perhaps set in a corner of a bathroom vanity. With so many color combinations there's bound to be a perfect one for every decor.

This little touch of yellow brings each blossom into focus.

Here are the same rocks we started with.

Which is real and which is rock? This is a great way to fill out any bare spots in your plantings.

*Painting Flowers on Rocks*

# How to Paint
# Mums

A number of flower varieties offer the challenge of capturing layered and overlapping petals; among them are zinnias, carnations, marigolds, dahlias and, my choice, mums. Even mums come in a variety of forms. Some have tight, mounded flower heads like cushions, while others are so loosely configured as to resemble daisies. The kind I've chosen falls somewhere in between these two extremes.

When it comes to color, few flowers can match the mum for pure dazzle. They light up autumn with their rich array of bronzes and golds, luxurious purples and mauves, even snowy whites with a blush of soft yellow tingeing the centers. After some experimentation, I settled on a deep red shaded with burgundy.

Both fieldstones and rounded river rocks can make great mums. Rocks with flat bases that allow them to stand alone are preferable, but these pieces will look equally attractive propped against a wall or entryway. My chosen rocks include two angular fieldstones whose shapes suggest compact containers below flowing foliage, along with one plump river rock whose size and bowl-shaped bottom make it ideal as a decorative centerpiece. Whether you choose a fieldstone or a river rock, look for one that is at least 8″ to 9″ (20.3cm to 22.9cm) tall so your mantel of blossoms will be close to life size.

## What You'll Need

- Patio Paint acrylics in Wrought Iron Black, Sprout Green, Geranium Red, Cloud White, Sunflower Yellow, Honest Copper, Pot O' Gold, Sunshine Yellow, Pinecone Brown and Summer Sky Blue
- assorted brushes, including a no. 0 or 1 script liner, a no. 6 filbert, small round brushes and large to medium flat brushes
- chalk or white charcoal pencil

Think big when it comes to mums—these dramatic flowers look best when executed on rocks that are at least 8″ to 9″ (20.3cm to 22.9cm) tall.

The layout will depend on the individual rock, but the most important element is to have lots of round and oval flowers clustered over the top half of the rock.

My rock has a simple shape that's slightly wider at the top.

# 1 Layout

Determine how big your container or bowl should be and sketch that dividing line first. The exact size may depend on the rock you choose, but try to keep the emphasis on the plant by making the container no more than a third of the total surface. The rock for this project measures 10″ (25.4cm) across the widest point and nearly 9″ (22.9cm) at the highest, while the bowl measures 2¾″ (7cm) high.

After marking the rim of the container, paint the entire upper surface in black mixed with just enough Sprout Green to soften it. When that coat dries, use a piece of chalk or white charcoal pencil to sketch the blossoms and foliage. Larger blooms will be more dramatic (and easier to paint), so make each flower at least 2″ (5.1cm) across. Draw some flowers nearly round while making others more oval, as though foreshortened.

Vary the sizes and overlap blossoms in many places for a more lifelike appearance. In addition, place several tightly closed and blossoming buds among the fully open ones. Fill in the lower portions with stems and leaf shapes, allowing a few leaves to droop over the edge of the container. Remember to sketch these elements on all the rock's surfaces: front, sides and back.

Create a dark background for the flower portion of your piece.

Flower heads should vary in size and shape. Allow several flowers to overlap, and include some tight buds and budding flowers.

A sample layout.

*Painting Flowers on Rocks*

## 2 Paint the Foliage

Because the petals give these flowers irregular edges, it's easier to paint in the foliage first. Use a script liner brush and mix just enough white into Sprout Green to make a slightly toned-down green that shows up well against the dark background. Paint in the stems first, leaving narrow spaces of dark paint showing between the edge of the container and the stems to suggest shadowing. Vary the angles of the stems, curving some more than others, and have a few smaller stems branching off the main ones.

To fill in the leaves, switch to a filbert or small round brush. Mums have somewhat ragged looking leaves, with larger ones at the bottom hanging down at various angles, and smaller, more perky leaves studding the upper portions of the stems. Use these leaves and parts of leaves to fill much of the space, leaving only scraps of dark undercoat for contrast.

## 3 Paint the Flower Shapes

Use a medium flat brush to mix the base color for these mums. Begin with Geranium Red and add small amounts of black until you reach a very deep burgundy shade. Fill in every flower head with this color. Make these circles correspondingly smaller for buds. Partially open buds are round along the bottom, with four or five individual petals fanning out from the top.

When all the flower heads are filled, add more black to your original mixture until the burgundy is almost but not quite black. Daub a smaller circle of this darker color in the center of each round blossom and nearer the top of each oval.

Start with a framework of stems using your script liner . . .

. . . then begin adding leaves.

This deep burgundy color serves to set off the actual petals.

A side view illustrates just how thickly the flower heads cover the top half of the rock.

Adding an even darker center will dramatically accentuate the tiny petals there.

## 4 Paint the Flower Petals

Use a no. 6 filbert brush to create the outside sets of petals. Mix two parts Sunflower Yellow with one part Geranium Red to produce a reddish orange shade that stands out from the deep base color of your flower heads. Start with the flowers on the side of your rock designated as the back. This will give you the opportunity to perfect your technique before detailing your primary side. Begin just within the circle of dark base, pulling your first elongated oval petal shape out so it's half inside and half outside the circle. These outer petals should be slightly longer along the bottom of the circle and shorter around the top.

Allow some petals to slant or extend farther than others, creating a profile that is slightly irregular. Next, move inside the first set and make a second row of petals. Start at the bottom, making these petals in the shape of ovals laid on their sides so as to appear foreshortened. Center them between the spaces of the outside petals. Leave narrow edges of dark base showing between

*Painting Flowers on Rocks*

each of these oval petals to keep them separate and distinct. As you move toward the upper side, gradually allow the petals to lengthen until they begin to overlap the outside set at the upper reaches of the circle. Subsequent sets are painted the same way, but in a slightly smaller size (switch to a smaller brush, or turn your filbert and use the edge). As you near the center, use the tip of a script liner to create a series of very small upright petals. For buds, add a few strokes of this lighter color along their top halves. For budding flowers, simply brighten the tips of the sprouting petals.

This same formula is repeated with every round flower head as you work your way over and around the surface of your rock. For ovals, use the illustration provided to place the petals. You may need to go over the petals with a second coat if they look too transparent.

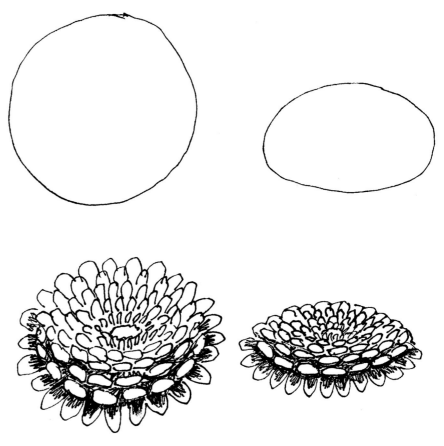

Petal conformation is altered by the angle of view.

Allow the outside set of petals to appear slightly irregular by varying petal sizes and angles.

Note how narrow spaces between these sets of petals help to define them.

*How to Paint Mums*

# 5 Create Shadows

Once the petals are in place, mix a deeper petal shade by adding a bit more Geranium Red and a trace of black. Add just enough water to give this pigment some of the transparency of a wash, and use it to add shadows to individual petals as shown. Making half-round shadows along the bottom half of the flower will give the petals their characteristic cupped shape. Shadow only the lower portion of each flower head to create the illusion of a light source above and to the right.

Switch to a smaller brush for the more delicate inner petals.

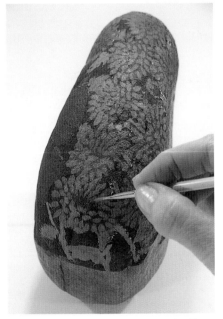

Continue to work your way methodically around the rock.

This shading not only indicates the way light might naturally fall on the flowers, but gives the petals a more dimensional look.

*Painting Flowers on Rocks*

# 6 Create Highlights

To brighten and separate each petal, mix a highlighting color made up of three parts Sunflower Yellow and a scant one part Geranium Red, making a shade that is visibly brighter than the original petal color. Use the point of your script liner to outline the tips of the petals. Highlights should be narrow and U-shaped on the lower side, reinforcing the cupped appearance made by previous shadowing. On the upper right side, stroke highlighting down from the petals' tips into their centers, again giving the impression of a strong light source above them. A touch of highlighting on every petal will add immeasurably to the look of these flowers.

Highlight the lower petals just along their outer edges.

Suffuse the upper petals with this lighter color.

Accents of Sunflower Yellow should be used sparingly—on just a few petals per flower head.

I'm using Honest Copper for my planter, but silver or gold metallics may be substituted.

This white line is just underpainting to help the next color stand out.

See how bright this gold rim looks.

## 7 Paint the Brass Container

Use a large brush to cover the entire container area with Honest Copper, being careful to paint around any overlapping leaves. If you have a very dark rock, it may take two coats to get solid coverage. When that paint is dry, use your script liner and white paint to highlight the top edge of the container all the way around, again skipping the overlapping leaves. When that dries, switch to Pot O' Gold and go over the rim again, creating the bright look of a gleaming metal edge.

## 8 Leaf Details

When the paint is dry, erase any remaining chalk guidelines using a damp towel to lift or wipe them away. Next, mix a deeper shade of green by adding a little black and a touch of Summer Sky Blue to the original green shade used to fill in the leaves. Use this color to run a line of shadow down the stems along the left side, then add feathery shading to the left or lower side of each leaf. Darken any parts of the leaves that are directly below flower heads. For variety, other leaves may be shaded along their top halves, leaving the tapered ends plain, or along the lower halves away from your established light source. Some leaves may appear lightly shadowed while others are mostly in shadow.

To highlight leaves, start again with your original leaf color, lightening it a shade or two with some Sunshine Yellow. Use your script liner to create a delicate set of veins and to add highlighting to the upper edges of many, but not all, of the leaves.

In looking over my array of foliage, I decided that too much dark base still showed. Therefore, I used the original leaf color, darkened just slightly with black, to tuck small leafy fragments wherever needed as fillers.

*Painting Flowers on Rocks*

Before detailing the leaves, use a damp cloth to wipe or rub away any remaining traces of the chalk layout.

Use deeper green shadows to push the foliage into the background, particularly under your flowers.

Can you see how a dark margin between the stems and rim pushes the foliage back while allowing the pot to stand out?

Concentrate these delicate highlighting lines on the sides of the stems and leaves consistent with your established light source.

Only when my leaves were finished did I see that adding a few leafy remnants would help fill out the foliage. Paint them in a medium green without shadows or highlights.

# 9 Finishing Touches

To give the brass container more sheen, use a large flat or round brush to add curving smears of gold to either side, simulating reflections. Then, with the tip of your script liner, dot small, tightly clustered Sunshine Yellow centers on each flower head. Dampen a small round brush before picking up a tipful of Pinecone Brown. Dilute the pigment enough to create the appearance of smudgy, translucent brown shadows on the container wherever leaves are overhanging. Confine these to the left sides, consistent with your imaginary light source.

Switch to a script liner and mix a tiny amount of Sprout Green with an even smaller amount of black. Use this to outline the left sides of the overhanging leaves, helping to lift them away from the shadows you just added.

Now look your mum over from every side to make sure you have detailed and finished all the flowers and leaves. Look for petals that could be neatened or redefined, and for areas where a bit more shadowing would create more visual interest. Finally, a light coat of acrylic spray will enrich the colors and protect the surface. Glue a scrap of felt to the bottom of the rock to protect furniture if you plan to display the rock indoors.

To paint yellow or gold mums, start with an undercoat of deep tan or orange-brown. For white flowers, make the undercoat a medium gray softened with Sunflower Yellow.

Gold smudges act as reflections to emphasize the curves of my brass bowl.

These small, irregular yellow centers give the flowers their focal points.

*Painting Flowers on Rocks*

Shadows beneath these overhanging leaves help lift them away from the brass surface. Outlining keeps the leaf edges distinct.

The same rocks shown at the beginning now transformed into glorious fall flowers.

Painting Flowers on Rocks

# How to Paint a
# Wreath of Roses

Many beginning painters are intimidated by roses, probably because they present so many different, often random looking, combinations of petal shapes. By breaking these shapes down into simple, easy-to-follow patterns, I hope to help you feel more comfortable and more confident. On the other hand, if you have already mastered rose painting, feel free to substitute your own style when painting them.

The climbing roses in my garden inspired this opulent design. I love the old-fashioned charm and subtle shadings of roses in full bloom. A rounded fieldstone or flat river rock makes a perfect surface for creating a rose wreath to display just as it is or to frame a family name, street address or a welcome to visitors. Pieces created specifically for outdoor display should always be made with paints designed to resist weathering.

Wreath rocks work best when they are fairly flat, and they don't need to be perfectly round. I occasionally come across a water-tumbled rock whose edges have been worn smooth, but rugged fieldstones are more common. Sizes can vary widely, but beginners should start with a rock that is around 12″ (30.5cm) in diameter so the roses won't look cramped. If you can't find one that big, it's better to cut down on the number of roses rather than trying to make them smaller.

The rock I've chosen is more oval than round, and the edges are quite angular. But it has a nice flat surface and is thick enough to stand alone. Thinner rocks can be propped up against a wall or porch post. Always scrub your rock before proceeding.

What these rocks have in common are their more or less round shapes and flat surfaces. When using a smaller rock, make fewer roses rather than smaller ones.

I like the generous size of the rock I chose, even though it's far from perfectly round.

Start with a deep blue base coat made by combining Summer Sky Blue and black. Paint the sides of your rock, then move to the main surface and create a wide circular frame.

Add more blue to your mixture, lightening it a shade, and continue to fill in the rock surface using circular strokes.

Lighten straight blue paint with white to create a milky blue. Fill in the very center of the rock, leaving an unpainted circle around it. Mix a brushful of deeper blue into the milky blue and fill in the remaining surface. Use a damp brush to blend wherever colors meet.

# 1 Create a Dramatic Backdrop

While a wreath of roses can be painted on any color background you wish, a deep base coat is a dramatic way to make the wreath stand out. Since many of the projects in this book start with dark green, let's try something different. Using a large dampened brush, pour out a generous amount of black and add enough Summer Sky Blue to create a shade slightly darker than navy blue. Apply this color to the entire outer portion of the rock face, including any sides that will show when the rock is standing or propped up. Work in toward the center, creating a circular frame. Pour out more Summer Sky Blue and add a heaping brushful to your black-blue mixture, lightening it a shade. Blend this color into the edges of the darker blue with scrubbing strokes as you work another inch or so toward the center.

Clean your brush and mix Summer Sky Blue with enough white to lighten it to a bright, milky blue. Fill in the very center of your rock with this color, leaving an unpainted circle surrounding it. Then dip a brushful of the milky blue into the blue used for the second ring, and mix the two together before applying this color to the remaining unpainted ring. Rinse your brush and use the moistened (but not dripping) bristles in tight scrubbing circles to blend away any lines where differing shades meet, so the overall effect will be one of subtle gradation from dark to light with no clearly defined borders. Whether you choose to paint a blue background or try some other color, starting with a deeper color at the outside edges and blending inward to a lighter shade will give your rock an eye-catching backdrop designed to set off roses to perfection.

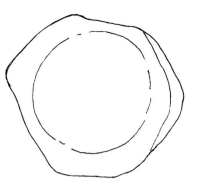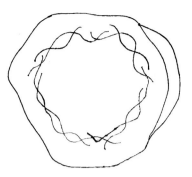

The vine layout in simple steps.

## 2 Sketch the Wreath Design

Use a white charcoal pencil to create your initial layout. Here is the opportunity to round out the overall appearance of your rock by moving in a few inches from the outside edges and creating a more uniform circular framework regardless of the irregularities of the rock itself.

Sketch the underlying rose vines with sets of overlapping and intertwining wavy lines that curve in segments, none extending longer than one-third of the way around the rock.

## 3 Paint the Rose Vines

Use a script liner and Fern Green with an added touch of Pinecone Brown to soften and brighten the color. Allow the ends of the vines to taper to points. Let them dry before adding flower heads.

Use a white charcoal pencil to sketch the curving vines in overlapping segments.

Don't worry about painting these vines in perfectly—many of them will be covered by flowers.

Center circles in various sizes amid the vines as shown, keeping them slightly smaller than the rose patterns provided.

Use a large brush to quickly fill in the dark base color of the roses.

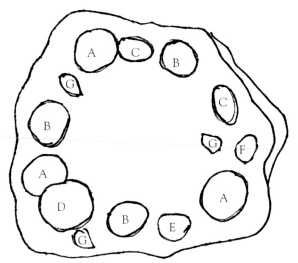

# 4 Sketch the Rose Layout

When sketching in the round rose shapes, make them at least 2″ (5.1cm) in diameter, but less than 3″ (7.6cm), and vary their placement for a naturally random look. For instance, cluster two or three roses together in one area, while leaving other roses to stand alone. Also vary the sizes of individual roses around the wreath to avoid a boring, overly structured look. One way to add variety is to place a few rosebuds or partially opened blooms among the full-blown blossoms. As you work to fit this design onto your rock, feel free to rub away your sketch marks and start over until you are satisfied with your composition.

# 5 Underpaint the Flower Heads

As with mums, starting with a deep base color beneath the flower heads creates the illusion of depth. For pink roses mix two parts Geranium Red with one part Woodland Brown. Use a large round or flat brush to fill in the circular rose shapes all around the wreath. If you are going to transfer the petal patterns (see step 6), keep these circles slightly smaller than the finished roses

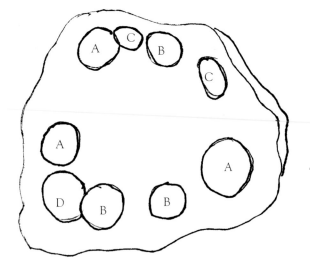

The basic rose layout, and one with buds and budding blossoms.

*Painting Flowers on Rocks*

will be. Also, fill in the smaller shapes of the buds and budding blossoms. The first coat may not completely cover the deep blue base or the vines, but they'll be covered in subsequent steps. Let this coat dry thoroughly.

Rinse out your brush and apply a second coat of straight Geranium Red to each flower head, leaving an open circle of the darker color uncovered in the center of each.

# 6 Transfer the Rose Patterns

If you like to draw, try sketching the rose petal patterns freehand when the underpainting has dried. If not, place a sheet of tracing or other lightweight paper over the petal patterns and copy the outlines. Turn the paper over and use the side of your white charcoal pencil to coat these lines. Then place the design, charcoal side down, so it covers the corresponding underpainted circle. Use a sharp pencil to transfer the design, transferring all the roses before you begin painting to avoid smudging damp paint. Reuse the same patterns as shown, reapplying white charcoal, then turning the pattern to transfer it in an altered position.

Make sure the previous coat is dry before adding a wide circle of straight red. Leave the center dark.

A

B

C

D

E

F

G

Rose petal pattern templates, labeled to illustrate placement on the basic rose layout on page 106.

*How to Paint a Wreath of Roses*

## 7 Rose Petal Pointers

Begin by mixing pale pink paint, adding one part red to four parts white. Use a ⅜-inch (10mm) angle shader for the larger petals, a ¼-inch (6mm) angle shader for the middle petals and a script liner for the narrowest ones. Before painting on your rock, practice using these brushes to make graceful curving shapes on a piece of paper. This will help you loosen up and also give you a feel for what you can do with these brushes. Remember that you can always repaint the base color and start over if you aren't happy with your first attempt, so there's no reason to be fearful.

## 8 Paint the Outside Petals

Place the brush edge even with the top end of your first petal and pull a narrow line. Slowly turn the brush counterclockwise, fitting it to the width of the petal and keeping the short bristle end even with the edge of the outside curve. When the brush fills the widest section of petal, stop turning until the petal begins to narrow again. Then resume turning the brush in the same counterclockwise direction until the line of the bristles is once again even with the tapering end of the petal. Smoothly lift your brush to create a tapering end.

Move on to whichever outside petal feels most natural, and continue filling petals using the twisting of your brush to create these sweeping strokes. To keep each petal well defined, leave edges of deep red base coat uncovered around them. If you do accidentally paint over one of these dark edges, go back with your script liner and replace it, using a mixture of red and brown.

## 9 Paint the Middle and Inside Petals

Paint the petals in the middle of your rose the same way, but use a smaller angle shader, taking care to leave margins of base coat around each petal. Continue working toward the center of the rose. There, switch to a script liner to create the narrow lines that represent the small inner circle of petals.

## 10 Blend and Shade the Rose Petals

Once your initial petal shapes have dried, mix a deeper shade of pink using one part white and one part Geranium Red. With a small round brush, apply this deeper pink along the inside halves of all the outside and middle petals. Use the dampened end of a cotton swab to blend this pink into the paler shade of pink so there are no hard edges. Lightly tint the centers with this deeper pink, but pat with a clean cotton swab to pick up some of the pigment. Allow this deeper pink to dry.

## 11 Deepen the Shadows With Red Tint

As a last touch, use plain Geranium Red, watered down to the consistency of a wash, to soften the stark differences between the defining lines of dark base coat and the paler shades of the petals. This red tint can be applied with either a small brush or a swab, but do keep a dry swab on hand to pick up excess paint and to soften away any harsh contrasts.

You may need to experiment with how much water and paint are needed to create a transparent tint that is still bright enough to serve as a buffer between the lighter and darker shades of your rose. Because the middle and innermost petals are recessed, it is natural that these areas should seem darker, so tint these petals all the way to the very edges.

## 12 Highlight the Petals

To finish detailing each rose, use a script liner and paint so pale a pink that it is nearly white to brighten petal edges that seem to need more definition. Vary the width of these highlighting lines, blending the widest ones into the surrounding petals.

Learn to create sweeping petal strokes so your petals will look more natural.

A. Petal pattern transferred and ready to paint.

B. Fill in the outer petals first.

C. Leave dark margins between the petals for definition.

D. Mix a deeper shade of pink to shade half the width of every petal along the inside edge. Use a moist cotton swab to soften and blend.

E. Water down straight red paint and use it to tint the innermost quarter of the width of each inside edge. In the center of the rose, tint the entire cluster of petals.

F. Mix a very pale pink (almost white) to highlight the outer edge of every petal. Use a script liner and vary the width of the highlighting lines for interest.

*How to Paint a Wreath of Roses*

Steps for creating buds and budding blossoms.

Leaves help frame and set off your finished roses.

Use an angle shader and Fern Green to fill in the leaves.

# 13 Buds and Budding Blossoms

Buds can be finished in just a few simple steps. Stroke your light pink petal color over the base-coated shape, leaving a trace of the base showing at the tip. When this paint dries, apply a bit of red wash to create the look of a shadowed underside. Use the tip of your script liner and a bit of very light pink to add the appearance of a tightly furled petal.

For budding blossoms, follow the same steps used to detail full-blown roses, starting with pink petals defined by edges of dark base coat. Use deeper pink and red tint to add shadows, and finish with a few spare touches of highlighting.

As you work your way around the wreath, you may feel that some of your roses are not as successful as others. While there is always the option of re-painting them, you may find that by the time you've detailed all the roses, any defects will have become less noticeable.

# 14 Sketch the Leaves

Leaves can be used to help balance and pull together the overall composition of your wreath. Use your white charcoal pencil to tuck leaves around and between your roses, both along the outside edges of the wreath and in the center. These leaves should be noticeably larger than your rosebuds. Point them in a variety of directions for a random and natural look.

*Painting Flowers on Rocks*

Leaf details.

# 15 Paint and Detail the Leaves

Fill in your leaf shapes using an angle shader and Fern Green. Using your script liner, extend skinny, little stems from the wreath to your buds and budding blossoms, attaching them with characteristic tapering green sepals.

Because the flowers are complex, keep your leaves simple and decorative. Mix a bit of black into your green to darken it, and use this to add a narrow spine down each leaf. Add a set of small, curving ribs to the lower side of each leaf, too.

Now mix a highlighting shade by adding a small amount of white to straight Fern Green. Use this to create a paler set of ribs on the other side of all the leaves, and to add a highlighting edge along the leaf on that side. With the same pale green, go around your wreath adding highlights to one side of every stem that is showing. Since this is a round piece, it doesn't matter where the imaginary light source is, so long as these lines seem consistent.

That completes the piece, unless you'd like to add something to the center. I created my wreath for our pastor and his wife, adding their name to personalize it. Just for fun, I painted a different design on the other side of the rose wreath, using an autumn leaf theme.

Attach buds and budding blossoms with narrow stems. Enclose the bud with three short green sepals. For budding blossoms, make these sepals larger while appearing to be peeled back.

Add pale green highlights to the stems.

The completed rose wreath.

# More Ideas . . .

Individual roses can also be painted on smooth round rocks using the same basic painting techniques. They make attractive paperweights and desk art, or can be arranged in a bowl to serve as a centerpiece.

For a different look, I painted a wreath of autumn leaves on the reverse side.

Here are the rocks shown earlier, now ready to grace the doorsteps of several friends.

You can create smaller rose rocks using the same techniques.

This lovely double rose was painted by a friend under my direction. It was her first rose and now sits proudly on her desk.

Painted by Karen Cunningham

Changing background and rose colors will yield a completely different look.

When painting smaller rocks, cut down on the number of roses rather than making them smaller.

*How to Paint a Wreath of Roses*

Painting Flowers on Rocks

# How to Paint a
# Flower Basket

An arrangement of mixed blooms is a time-honored way to beautify a room. Here's a striking new way to celebrate your love of fresh flowers without them wilting or dropping their petals.

Any occasion that calls for the gift of fresh flowers might also be a perfect time to bestow one of these delightfully original works of art. Flower baskets make breathtaking centerpieces and accents. They also offer you the opportunity to paint your own particular floral favorites. These baskets can be done in absolutely any size, too, from delicate miniatures to as large a piece as you may be inspired to try.

The plump contours of river rocks are perfect for flower baskets. For this demonstration, I've selected a rock whose shape is so suggestive of a round basket that it takes very little imagination to envision it. But if you don't have access to such river-tumbled rocks, don't despair. Many fieldstones and chunky rocks offer shapes that can be used to create quite dramatic pieces.

For your first attempt, I recommend using a fairly good-sized rock—one with room to make your blooms large and showy. My rock is just over 10″ (25.4cm) as measured from side to side and about 9″ (22.9cm) tall. It has a flat bottom, which allows it to sit, and a pleasing symmetry—certainly an important element for the bottom or basket portion of the rock.

## What You'll Need

- Patio Paint acrylics in Pine Green, Wrought Iron Black, Woodland Brown, Cloud White, Sunshine Yellow, Sunflower Yellow and Geranium Red
- Apple Barrel acrylics in Dutch Blue and Wild Iris
- assorted brushes, including a large flat brush, a no. 0 or 1 script liner, a ⅛-inch (3mm) angle shader, a ⅜-inch or ½-inch (10mm or 13mm) angle shader and several medium and small round brushes or filberts
- white charcoal pencil

Any of these rocks would be a good candidate to become a basket of flowers. The rock I'll be painting is to the left and in the rear.

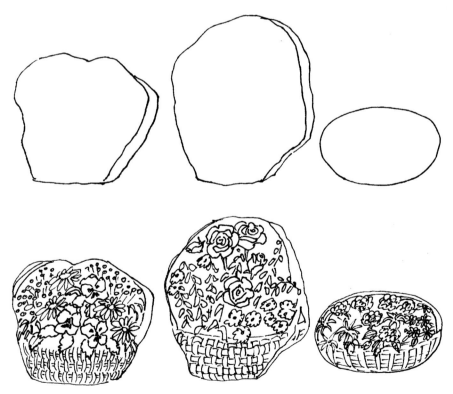

Many more rock shapes can be used—and many other styles of baskets, too.

# 1 Basket Layout

Although the woven texture of the basket is a vital ingredient, the flowers are the real focal point. On my rock the height of the basket is only 2½" (6.4cm), yet it doesn't look skimpy. As a general rule, the basket should take up no more than a third of the surface area on each side.

Use a white charcoal pencil to sketch in the basket rim, allowing this line to curve just slightly to suggest roundness. Sketch a set of parallel lines over the top of the rock from end to end to form the handle. My handle is not quite 1" (2.5cm) wide.

# 2 Paint the Base Coats

Use a large flat brush to cover the upper portion of your rock with a mixture of Pine Green and black, creating a dramatic backdrop for your flowers. Paint right up to the edges of the handle guidelines.

Rinse your brush and switch to Woodland Brown to fill in the basket portion of the rock, leaving the handle unpainted for now. Let this paint dry before going on.

This slightly curved line establishes the rim of the basket.

This deep green base coat serves as a dramatic backdrop.

Leave the handle unpainted for now.

Fill in the basket bottom with dark brown.

## 3 Paint the Basket Weave

There are many different patterns of basket weave, and later you may want to try other designs. This pattern is one of the easiest, though, so it's a good place to start. First, sketch in the uprights, making them between 1″ and 1½″ (2.5cm and 3.8cm) apart. To ensure that your weaving will come out evenly, you must have an odd number of uprights. It may be helpful to measure and mark lines around the diameter with your white charcoal pencil to make sure that you end with an odd number.

Using your ⅛-inch (3mm) angle brush, mix white paint with just enough Sunflower Yellow to make a soft ivory. Stroke in the vertical uprights by first painting a straight narrow line in the center, running from the rim to the bottom of the rock. Move to the left and make your second upright, this time curving the bottom half of the line slightly toward the center. Move the same distance to the left again, and make a matching line. Continue these evenly spaced lines until you are halfway around the left side. Now return to the right side of the center and fill in another set of lines, again curving the base of the first one or two uprights gently toward the center. Continue around your rock with these evenly spaced lines until you reach the previous set.

To give a finished look to the edge of the basket rim, place your brush at an angle and press on a series of short, matching strokes along the top edge of the basket all the way around. Next, using the same small angle shader, begin making the horizontal weaving lines. Leave a ¼″ (6mm) space between the basket rim and your first curving line. Start midway between one set of uprights and end the line in the center of the next set. Drop down, leaving a space the width of one brushstroke, and

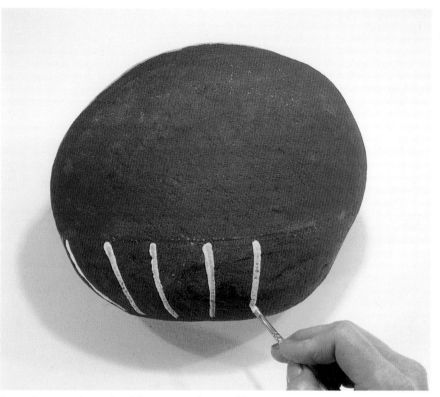

Paint the vertical uprights following evenly spaced lines.

Add matching strokes to the top edge for a finished look.

Paint the horizontal weaving lines, leaving ¼″ (6mm) between the basket rim and your first curving line.

Curving lines create the illusion of a woven basket.

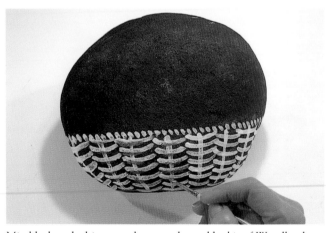

Mix black and white to make gray, then add a bit of Woodland Brown to warm it. Add enough water so the paint flows smoothly, and lightly shadow the bottoms of all the horizontal weaving.

continue with this series of curved lines until you reach the bottom of the rock.

Start your next set of horizontals along the edge of the rim, with the end resting atop the end of your very first horizontal line. Each subsequent curving line is then tucked between the ends of the neighboring set to create the illusion of being interwoven. The odd number of uprights ensures that your weaving will come out perfectly after you've painted around to your starting place.

# 4 Shade the Basket Weave

Mix a small amount of black and white to make a medium shade of gray, and add a touch of brown to warm it. Use the same small angle brush, dampened enough to dilute the paint so, while not as watery as a wash, it's still loose enough to stroke on smoothly. Darken the lower edge of every horizontal line as well as the ends of the lines that appear to tuck under the neighboring sets. Use a bit of black paint to touch up slanted trim lines around the basket rim to keep them distinct from the weaving lines below.

*Painting Flowers on Rocks*

## 5 Paint the Handle

With the same ivory basket color, fill in the handle. Where the handle meets the basket, stop just short of the rim so a narrow margin of dark base coat separates the two elements.

## 6 Lay Out the Design of the Flowers

I find it helpful to make preliminary sketches on paper before settling on a design. With several nursery catalogs providing inspiration, I decided on large lilies for the foreground, along with multicolored gaillardias, or blanket flowers, and some simple white cosmos. For height and variety, I included a backdrop of tall, spiky flowers, selecting a variety of delphiniums with simple, bell-shaped florets.

Copy the basic design onto the surface of your rock with your white charcoal pencil. Be sure your blossoms are large enough to fill the entire area allotted to them, and allow the lilies to overlap the edges of the basket, integrating the two elements.

While decisions about the overall design of this arrangement were made from foreground to background, for painting it's easier to start at the back and paint forward. You can work on both the front and rear sides of your rock at once or complete one side at a time.

Take your time with the handle to make it straight and even along the edges.

Too symmetrical.          Out of balance.          Naturally balanced.

When creating your own design, balance a few large flowers against more numerous but smaller ones and simple blossoms against complex types. Avoid too much symmetry; instead, seek to create a dynamic composition.

Begin by sketching your foreground flowers, add the middle ground, then fill in the background.

*Painting Flowers on Rocks*

When painting, it's easier to start at the back and work forward. Note how the tips of my flower spikes overlap the edge of the basket handle for an added hint of dimension.

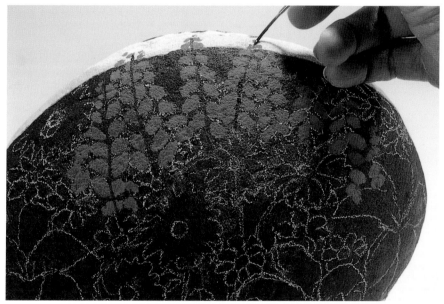

Once the outside florets are painted, add a dark stem up the center.

## 7 Spikey Blue Flowers

Select a round brush that most closely matches the size of the individual floret shapes in your design. Begin with a small puddle of Dutch Blue paint and add increments of Wild Iris until you reach a deep shade of purple-blue. Create florets by simply laying your paint-laden brush against the rock at a slight angle to the stem of the spike, brush tip down. Work your way up the spike along the same side, making each subsequent floret smaller by laying down less and less of the brush until, at the tip of the stem, the florets are little more than dots. Make a mirror-image set along the other side of the spike, but offset them so they alternate rather than match up. Although it barely shows, don't neglect the flower spike above the lily on the far left. When this paint is dry, use a script liner and Pine Green to paint in the center stem.

Add just enough white to lighten the blue floret color a shade, and make a third more sparse set of blossoms up the center of the spike, tilting some to the left and some to the right as they become smaller and smaller. Repeat until all the spikes are covered with florets. To highlight them, lighten your blue one more shade and lightly stroke the tip of your brush along the upper side of each floret. Switch to a smaller round brush and use black paint to add a dark spot at the end of each floret, creating the look of a neat, round opening. These dark spots should become smaller as the florets shrink in size and stop before you reach the smallest florets at the very top.

Space the florets farther apart down the center so traces of the spiky stem show.

Highlighting the florets with a touch of light blue really helps to round them out.

These dark centers give the flowers their characteristic bell shape.

*Painting Flowers on Rocks*

# 8 Paint the White Cosmos

Thoroughly clean your round brush, then paint in the seven plump petals that will form the cosmos flower head, leaving narrow spaces between each petal to help define them. I included one cosmos in side view for variety; several other flowers will be only partially visible behind the still-to-be-painted lilies. We'll come back and detail the cosmos blossoms later.

# 9 Paint the Gaillardias

Not only are these flowers dramatic looking, they are fun and easy to do. Start by placing equal amounts of Sunshine Yellow and Geranium Red side by side so their edges meet. Use a ½-inch (13mm) angle shader to pick up both colors equally. Set the short end of the angle shader close to the edge of the center circle sketched earlier, and simply press lightly to create a two-toned petal. You can probably paint at least two petals before you need to reload as you slowly work your way around the outside of the flower center. Make sure you adjust the direction of the brush with each petal so they radiate out evenly all the way around.

A sprinkling of crisp, white cosmos complement the vivid blue flowers, and their simple shape is a pleasing contrast to the more complex spikes. Turning one cosmos sideways adds a lifelike touch.

Press gaillardia petals into place like sun rays. Allow the petals of the top two flower heads to overlap.

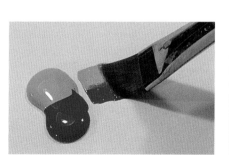

Place your two colors side by side and pick up equal amounts of each with the edge of your angle brush.

# 10 More Details

While you still have Sunshine Yellow on your palette, use a small round brush to add tidy yellow centers to all your cosmos. To complete the gaillardias, paint a narrow ring of Woodland Brown around the base of the petals. Fill the centers with a blend of Sunflower Yellow slightly toned down with Woodland Brown. Finally, use a script liner and Sunshine Yellow to add tiny, random looking dots of color to the dark brown rings.

Make these yellow centers small enough to leave a bit of dark base coat showing between them and their petals.

Use Woodland Brown to create a dark ring around the base of the petals.

Darken a drop of Sunflower Yellow with a trace amount of Woodland Brown and use this somber yellow to fill in the gaillardias' centers.

These tiny yellow dots are a small touch but they add to the realistic look of the flowers.

# 11 Paint the Lilies

Return to your ½-inch (13mm) angle shader and mix a peach shade using roughly five parts white, two parts Geranium Red and one part Sunshine Yellow. Paint in the three dominant petals, leaving a dark gap at the center. The pointed petal tips should curve uniformly downward. Add one slightly smaller petal between each of the first three, not quite touching the others to keep each distinct. Paint your second and third lilies the same way.

When all the lilies are painted, mix Geranium Red with a tiny amount of black to create a rusty red shade. Use your smallest angle shader to darken the very centers, stroking outward along the middle of each petal. Drybrush more of this rusty color along the outside edges of the petals as well, and add even more shading at the bases of the secondary petals.

Rinse your brush and switch to white paint with just a hint of Geranium Red to make it pale pink. Outline the edges of all the petals, again keeping your brush rather dry so these outlines have a soft, somewhat diffused appearance. At this point, I went back over my lilies with a few more touches of deeper shading on petals I missed earlier.

Create the top three petals first, then tuck the remaining three between them.

This deep, rusty color adds depth and dimension when used to shade the lilies.

A relatively dry brush gives these pale outlines a soft look while helping the lilies stand out.

## 12 Finishing Touches for Flowers

To make the freckles that decorate these lilies, mix a bit more black into Geranium Red to make maroon. Use the tip of your script liner to dot in these freckles, making some larger and more irregular while others are tiny specks. Concentrate them mainly in the middles, leaving the ends of the petals plain.

To add the stamen, mix a drop of Sunshine Yellow with an equal amount of white to make a pale, buttery color. Use your script liner to make four narrow lines that fan out from the center of each lily. Top each stamen with a teardrop-shaped stroke of burnt orange made by mixing a brushful of Geranium Red with one of Sunshine Yellow and toning it down with a bit of Woodland Brown.

## 13 Painting the Foliage

To fill in the remaining area of this bouquet, mix Pine Green with enough Sunshine Yellow to make a bright green. Paint in a set of narrow stems using your script liner. Begin these stems slightly above the edge of

Dark freckles and pale stamens with orange tips complete these flowers.

the basket, leaving a dark margin. For continuity, extend a couple stems up from behind the cosmos to join with the two highest gaillardia blossoms; also extend stems to the two tallest cosmos flowers to the right as well as the one that's turned sideways and the two tiny ball-shaped buds beside it.

Create a series of leaves and parts of leaves to fill in the spaces between and around the flowers. Have a few leaves hang down over the top of the basket. I also added a closed gaillardia bud for

more variety. To create shadows, mix a bit of black into your Pine Green. Use this to darken the base of any leaf directly below a flower and to add veins here and there. For highlights, mix more yellow into your original green and use it to bring out the edge of a leaf here or to emphasize a stem there.

If there are any traces of your original white charcoal sketch marks showing, this is a good time to rub them away as you are looking for areas that may need more detail.

Light green stems are the first step in filling in the foliage.

Leaf and bud details.

*Painting Flowers on Rocks*

# 14 Last Touches

Mix a drop of white with some black to make a soft gray, and use your script liner to create tiny lines of texture that radiate over the cosmos petals. And finally, use the same brush to add narrow brown lines along both edges of the basket handle, giving it the appearance of having some thickness rather than being paper thin. As always, a light spray of acrylic sealer will add more life to your colors.

While these baskets of mixed flowers may be challenging to paint, I think the stunning results are well worth the effort!

A few gray lines radiating out from the centers add the texture of small ridges to the cosmos petals.

Use a script liner and brown paint to create narrow lines along the basket handle to add depth.

The completed basket of flowers.

*How to Paint a Flower Basket*

# Index